REVOLUTIONARY RECOGNITION

Also Available from Bloomsbury

From Marx to Hegel and Back: Capitalism, Critique, and Utopia, ed. Victoria Fareld and Hannes Kuch
The Bloomsbury Companion to Marx, ed. Andrew Pendakis, Imre Szeman and Jeff Diamanti
Critical Theory and the Critique of Political Economy: On Subversion and Negative Reason, Werner Bonefeld
Georg Lukács's Philosophy of Praxis: From Neo-Kantianism to Marxism, Konstantinos Kavoulakos

REVOLUTIONARY RECOGNITION

RICHARD GUNN AND ADRIAN WILDING

BLOOMSBURY ACADEMIC
LONDON • NEW YORK • OXFORD • NEW DELHI • SYDNEY

BLOOMSBURY ACADEMIC
Bloomsbury Publishing Plc
50 Bedford Square, London, WC1B 3DP, UK
1385 Broadway, New York, NY 10018, USA

BLOOMSBURY, BLOOMSBURY ACADEMIC and the Diana logo are trademarks of
Bloomsbury Publishing Plc

First published in Great Britain 2021

Copyright © Richard Gunn and Adrian Wilding, 2021

Richard Gunn and Adrian Wilding have asserted their right under the Copyright,
Designs and Patents Act, 1988, to be identified as Authors of this work.

For legal purposes the Acknowledgements on p. xii constitute an extension
of this copyright page.

Cover design by Charlotte Daniels
Cover image: *The Fourth Estate (Il Quarto Stato)* by Giuseppe Pellizza da Volpedo (c. 1901)
(© The Picture Art Collection / Alamy Stock Photo)

All rights reserved. No part of this publication may be reproduced or transmitted
in any form or by any means, electronic or mechanical, including photocopying,
recording, or any information storage or retrieval system, without
prior permission in writing from the publishers.

Bloomsbury Publishing Plc does not have any control over, or responsibility for, any third-party websites referred to or in this book. All internet addresses given in this book were correct at the time of going to press. The author and publisher regret any inconvenience caused if addresses have changed or sites have ceased to exist, but can accept no responsibility for any such changes.

A catalogue record for this book is available from the British Library.

A catalog record for this book is available from the Library of Congress.

ISBN: HB: 978-1-3501-3739-4
ePDF: 978-1-3501-3740-0
eBook: 978-1-3501-3741-7

Typeset by Deanta Global Publishing Services, Chennai, India

To find out more about our authors and books visit www.bloomsbury.com
and sign up for our newsletters.

CONTENTS

Foreword by John Holloway vi
Acknowledgements xii

Introduction 1

1 Hegel's dangerous idea 5

2 Marx as thinker of recognition 31

3 Revolutionary or less-than-revolutionary recognition? 61

4 Mutual recognition in practice 83

5 Recognition's environment 107

Conclusion 133

Notes 141
References 159
Name & Subject Index 170

FOREWORD BY JOHN HOLLOWAY

Super! Exciting! I've just finished reading the book and I'm delighted. I knew I would like it – I've known Richard and Adrian for many years – but I didn't know I would find it so exciting.

What is so exciting about it? For me two things: the very notion of mutual recognition and then the way they follow the concept from Hegel to Marx to Occupy to commons to climate change, pausing on the way to criticize the liberal reformism of Taylor and Honneth.

Mutual recognition moves from being the key category in a learned but unorthodox reading of Hegel's *Phenomenology of Spirit* to being a key component in the rethinking of anti-capitalist revolution. For Hegel mutual recognition finds expression in the 'I that is We and We that is I' (1977: 110) that he saw in the revolutionary crowd at the height of the French Revolution. Marx and Engels expressed the same idea in the closing sentence of *Communist Manifesto* Part II, when they spoke of communism as 'an association, in which the free development of each is the condition for the free development of all' (Marx and Engels 1976b: 506).

For Hegel, history is a movement through various forms of false or contradicted recognition to reach a true mutual recognition. The master-slave dialectic sets the scene: neither slave nor master is recognized as a person. Each is 'recognized' through the role they occupy in the relation, or perhaps misrecognized or malrecognized, since their personhood is reduced to that role. This false or contradicted or malrecognition is not an error of perception, since recognition is constitutive: we are constituted by the recognition of others. The slave is reduced to being a slave through the master's (and his own) recognition of himself as such; the master too is reduced to being a master through the slave's (and his own) recognition of himself as such. Mutual recognition (and therefore our own fullness as people) can be realized only through the abolition of the master-slave relation, that is, of all relations of domination.

Much the same argument can be made in relation to Marx. In *Capital* he emphasizes on repeated occasions that the existence of the commodity reduces people to 'personifications' or 'character masks' as buyers or sellers. When the commodity is the labour power of the workers, here too the seller (the worker) and the buyer (the capitalist) are reduced to personifications of their location in the relation. They are pushed into roles as buyer or seller, worker or capitalist. Mutual recognition of people as people, with all the things they have in common and all their particularities, could come only with the overcoming of relations of domination and the formation of a society based on 'an association, in which the free development of each is the condition for the free development of all'.

This is a vastly oversimplified presentation of the notion of mutual recognition. What I really want to ask is how does this take us forward in our understanding of revolution, of the possibilities of radical social change? Richard and Adrian's book is enormously, excitingly ambitious. They want to bring the long-neglected Left-Hegelian tradition into the centre of current radical anti-capitalist movements like Occupy, the commons movement and the movement for climate justice. I think they are absolutely right to do so, but just how does the notion of mutual recognition help us?

For me the notion of mutual recognition adds a new dimension, or perhaps a new cutting-edge to Marx's concept of fetishism, which is at the centre of his critique of capitalism in *Capital*. The existence of our products as commodities leads to a fetishization or reification (Lukács) of social relations. I buy a car: this appears to be simply a relation between my money and the thing bought. Behind this, however, is a social relation, a relation between active subjects: a relation between my activity as a professor, for which I have been paid with money, and the work of the workers in who knows where, Japan, Korea, Mexico, who have made the car. The relation between me and the car workers is a social relation which exists in the form of a relation between things, in other words, a fetishized or reified relation.

How does it help us if we now add a reflection on recognition to this? My payment of money is a perverted act of recognition: I recognize the work that the workers have done so that I can drive around in safety and comfort. Behind the monetary transaction there is a subjacent we-ness. There is a coming together of their activity as car workers with my activity as a professor that enriches the world in some way. If we think of the relationship in terms of recognition, then a warmth comes into it. I want to shake their hands, thank them for the skill and care they applied in making the car so comfortable and safe. They, no doubt, would want to say to me, 'I found your foreword to the Gunn and Wilding book really motivating, I must tell my children about it this evening.' But of course, our mutual recognition does not happen in that way. I pay my money to the car dealer, or rather to the credit company; the workers receive their wage and have no interest in my existence, and that is that. There is a dreadful and violent malrecognition here that contradicts the potential richness and warmth of the subjacent we-ness. The contradiction is a strong one, between the world of mutual recognition that could be and the dead-killing thing-ness of the contradicted recognition in which we live.

Recognition is a flow. There is nothing fixed about the 'I that is We and We that is I': it is in constant movement as the 'I's change, as the 'We's change, as their relationship changes. For Hegel, it is the excitement of the revolutionary crowd. It is ephemeral, evanescent perhaps, it makes no claim on the future, pre-defines nothing. It is what Bloch, following Boethius and inspired by Goethe's *Faust*, calls the *nunc stans*, the perfect moment that reaches for eternity. It is Benjamin's *Jetztzeit*, now-time, a moment of unbearable intensity. The moment of mutual recognition is not necessarily short-lived; it is rather the breaking of any notion of duration, the rupture of the homogeneity of time. Richard Gunn once wrote, in a review of Bloch's *Principle of Hope*, that no one placed the stakes so high in their understanding of communism. But that is just what he and Adrian are doing in their insistence that communism is mutual recognition. That is what makes the book beautiful. Their mutual recognition is just as wildly ambitious as Bloch's *nunc stans* or Benjamin's *Jetztzeit*.

Wildly ambitious certainly, perhaps also wildly unrealistic for those of us whose senses have been dulled by the society in which we live. But perhaps that is not the point. For just as Benjamin's *Jetztzeit* is a scream against the deadening homogeneity of time that condemns us to tomorrow being a continuation of today and just as Bloch's *nunc stans* is the most intense expression of hope against the tick-tock of oppression, so mutual recognition is not just the expression of a possible communizing future but also and above all a movement-against its own contradicted existence. Or better, a movement-against its own contradicted existence. Hyphenated because the movement of mutual recognition can only be a negative movement, a movement-against, in a society that contradicts it. Even if we think of mutual recognition as having been realized, as apparently Hegel did in his own time, an immense silliness that has done much to undermine the dangerousness of his ideas, even then, it would have to be understood negatively as a constant movement-against the encroachment of its own institutionalization. Certainly in the present capitalist society, mutual recognition exists, to use Richard's classic and much-quoted phrase, 'in the mode of being denied', and therefore as struggle against its own denial.

Mutual recognition, then, is a flow that exists in the mode of being contradicted. What contradicts it is anything that blocks the flow. Any freezing that turns the water into ice, any coagulation or clotting that impedes the flow of blood. Richard and Adrian speak of role definitions as 'reified ice floes that are carried on recognition's tide' (p. 52). Hegel speaks of *geistige Massen*, spiritual masses, which I understand to mean massifications or coagulations in the flow of the spirit. To say that mutual recognition exists as contradicted means that it exists as coagulated, clotted, in spiritual masses. It exists as roles, as institutions, as definitions, as limits, as perimeters, as sects, as parties, as anything that converts the flow of becoming into the stasis of being. The 'I that is We and We that is I' never *is*: it flows. For the same reason, 'communism' is a nonsensical term: it makes sense only as a communizing.

Mutual recognition, as movement-against, is anti-identitarian. This is crucially important when we relate the concept to current struggles. Richard and Adrian say that 'political philosophy has never been closer to political reality' (p. 4). That is key to the powerful link between the earlier and the later chapters of the book. The earlier chapters focus on the concept of mutual recognition and the importance of the Left-Hegelian tradition, including Marx in that tradition, while the later chapters centre on the significance of that tradition for the practice of current struggles. The bridge is the critique of the abandonment of the Left-Hegelian-Frankfurt-School tradition by the later generation of the Frankfurt School, Honneth in particular. The argument flows beautifully and is very convincing. Mutual recognition, the abolition of hierarchies, the pursuit of horizontality and the attempt to listen to all voices in a movement, is indeed a central feature of radical struggles over the last twenty years or so, perhaps ever since the Zapatista uprising with its emphasis on 'dignity' as the central principle of organization and struggle. The idea of prefiguration is a reaching towards a mutually recognitive society through the creation of similarly recognitive organizing here and now. In that sense, Richard and Adrian are right to say that the Left-Hegelian tradition is at the centre of current struggles. Yet even here it is important to emphasize the negativity of the tradition, the fact that the movement of mutual recognition is a movement-against. Against the commodity form and the clotting that is inherent in that form. Against the dangers of encroaching identities, perimeters (sometimes tied to the notion of community), definitions, roles, never far from even the most exciting movements.[1] That is precisely why the notion of mutual recognition is so important to political practice, as restless, unceasing critique, as constant push against the obstacles that impede its flow.

To recover the force of 'mutual or revolutionary recognition' and with it Hegel's *Phenomenology* and the Left-Hegelian tradition and to place them in the centre of the current longings for a different world, where they are already – what a fabulously important project!

Read on. Or if you've skipped over this foreword, don't worry. The exciting part starts in the pages that follow.

ACKNOWLEDGEMENTS

This book has its origins in 1989, a year of revolutions, when Adrian enrolled in a course offered by Richard at Edinburgh University's Department of Politics on 'Hegel's *Phenomenology* and Political Theory'. Since that time, and never merely in the roles of teacher and student, the two have collaborated as equals and friends. Both Adrian and Richard happily acknowledge their great intellectual debt to each other. *Revolutionary Recognition* distils three decades of their collaboration. For their support during the writing of the book Adrian would also like to thank Ina and James. Richard thanks Michele for everything.

Introduction

Our book champions the notion of 'recognition [*Anerkennung*]'. In understanding a politics of emancipation, 'recognition' – so we urge – is the key. Mutual recognition (a term which we explain in due course) is the goal and rationale of revolution. Recognition is the theme which underlies critical theory and holds the route to revolution clear. In present-day society, individuals confront a world that has 'the character of being something external' – to quote Hegel (1977: 294) – and alienation is the result. Neoliberal thinking stifles political initiatives which bring the notion of a 'we' of individuals into play. A politics of recognition, or of mutual recognition more specifically, is a politics 'in, against and beyond capitalism', to borrow John Holloway's pregnant phrase (Holloway 2016).

In speaking of revolutionary recognition, our aim is to clear a space in which revolution's hope for an 'association' where 'the free development of each is the free development of all' – or, in Hegel's expression, an 'I that is We and We that is I' (1977: 110) – can be renewed.

Developments in capitalism are not, we think, the only reason why an emphasis on recognition is timely. Changes in the Left also foreground recognitive themes. During the nineteenth and most of the twentieth centuries, the Left hoped and dreamed and acted in broadly social democratic ways. Lenin's desideratum of an avant-garde party of professional revolutionaries increased the tempo of revolutionary struggles but left their statist and social democratic framework intact. Now, everything has changed. Since, roughly, 2011, revolutionary struggles have dispensed with social democracy and an exclusive focus on seizing parliamentary power. They have turned to a direct and much more fluid form of interaction. In doing so, they take up – sometimes implicitly, sometimes explicitly – the notion of mutual recognition we set out in this book. Present-day revolutionary theory for its part broadens the terms of debate. In the exchange between Lenin and Luxemburg in the early part of the twentieth century (the exchange which came to be known as the 'problem of organization'[1]), neither side acknowledged that organization may or must have a prefigurative dimension.[2] Later in the twentieth century, in the feminist movement especially, prefigurative thought and action became widespread – as did 'prefiguration' as a term.[3] In the more recent 'Occupy' movement of 2011-13, prefiguration became a central and explicit theme.[4] Today, the terms at issue in orthodox Marxism's 'problem of organization' have altered. In the movements that have flourished since 2011 not merely an emphasis on participatory democracy but themes of prefiguration and 'horizontal' democracy[5] go without saying. Gunn and Wilding's *Revolutionary Recognition* speaks for and attempts to strengthen this Marxist and, at the same time, anarchist trend.[6]

The argument in this book is both theoretical and practical. It begins in a theoretical vein, by considering the origins of the term 'recognition' in the philosophy of Hegel. Our reading of Hegel breaks new ground in emphasizing the radical, indeed revolutionary, implications of his understanding of this idea. From Hegel we turn to Marx who, we argue, took up Hegel's understanding of recognition, using it as a key weapon in his critique of capitalism. That Marx, like Hegel, was a thinker of recognition has received little attention in Marxist theorizing, an omission our book aims to redress. Our discussion then turns to present-day academic treatments of recognition. We argue that recent academic theory has, by and large, forgotten the term's original revolutionary meaning. Academic theory has drawn the concept's revolutionary sting. Here we underline something that a reader of our book must heed if they are to understand our argument. The recognition that Gunn and Wilding champion *is not* the largely reformist notion discussed today by Charles Taylor and Axel Honneth and academics who follow in their wake, but rather *recognition in its original revolutionary sense*. Our chapters on Hegel and Marx attempt to breathe fresh life into lines of argument which Honneth and present-day academia (discussed in Chapter 3) have diluted, downplayed or even opposed. Our book is, to this extent, an 'anti-Honneth' (to invoke the title though not the substance of a well-known Engelsian polemic).

In the second half of the book we turn from 'theory' to 'practice' and more directly political questions. Chapters 4 and 5 of our book explore what a practice of mutual (i.e. revolutionary) recognition may look like and discuss some of the political issues recognition raises. Recognition, we argue in Chapter 4, is the thread that connects the seemingly diverse ideas and ideals that guide revolutionary struggles today. It is a concept which makes sense of the global Left's rejection of social democratic politics and its turn to a politics of prefiguration. It is a term which allows the 'problem of organization' to be thought anew. In Chapter 4, we also consider various challenges to our idea that mutual recognition should be the rallying cry for the Left; in particular, the idea that no revolutionary movement can do without hierarchy, and that mutual recognition cannot work on a large scale.

The struggles of recent years have cast into relief fresh possibilities and scarcely imagined themes.[7] For the first time, radical social movements have made mutual recognition a direct and explicit aim. Can these movements, and their mutually recognitive heritage, be sustained and developed and extended? We believe that they can, and that the dominance of social democracy in radical thought is a thing of the past. 'Recognition', as an expression and a concept, is the term of the day.

In Chapter 5 we address one further key criticism that can be levelled at a notion of recognition – that it has little to say about how humans should treat the natural world. If mutual recognition occurs between humans, then what rationale does it give for protecting other species, ecosystems, the planet as such? We show ways in which this difficulty can be overcome and 'red' and 'green' struggles against capitalism can be united.

Though the final chapters of the book deal with more practical issues, ours is nevertheless a work that constantly looks to radical ideas from the history of political thought and demonstrates their topicality. One way of expressing our book's aim is to say, we attempt to renew the tradition of 'Left' (or 'radical' or 'Young') Hegelianism which Hegel's notion of recognition inaugurates and to which Marx belongs. We attempt to breathe fresh life into a position which, in the neoliberal period, has been neglected and hollowed out. Yet besides attempting to renew a school of thought, however vital, we see our discussion in political terms. The Left-Hegelian line of thought which we attempt to renew here is, we believe, vital to struggle today. Political philosophy has never been closer to political reality. As a result, if the book is found convincing, Left Hegelianism will be renascent and terms from Hegel's *Phenomenology* will be on political activists' lips. The social world will turn on its axis. All this is for the future: for now, it is enough to introduce a reader to a line of thought that has, in neoliberal times, been marginalized but which has revolutionary strength.

1

Hegel's dangerous idea

Why should revolutionaries read Hegel? What does the Left have to learn from Hegel's philosophy today? If we follow the tradition of dialectical materialism which had such enormous influence on the revolutionary Left in the twentieth century, it seems Hegel has little to tell us. At best, Hegel theorized a 'dialectic' whose form was taken over by Marx and Engels (and Lenin) and rendered 'scientific' by shedding its 'idealist' content. For the dialectical materialists, Hegel was a thinker 'standing on his head' (see Engels 1946: 39) who needed to be 'put back on his feet' if anything useful were to be gleaned from his thought. Our own position has absolutely nothing in common with these assumptions. For a reader to understand our argument about recognition, these assumptions – or better, prejudices – about Hegel (and Marx) must be left at the door.

A second prejudice bars the way to understanding Hegel's import for the Left, and that is an assumption about how Hegel's various writings are to be seen. For many academic readers of Hegel today his writings form a coherent life's work – a *system* – where the fundamental outlook remained unchanged throughout his lifetime. While the assumption of the coherence of Hegel's various writings has remained influential in academia, controversy about how Hegel's 'earlier' and 'later' writings relate has never been far away. Soon after Hegel's death in 1831, followers of his philosophy divided into two schools: the 'Old Hegelians' who favoured a systematic view of his work and who sought to reconcile his teachings with Christian orthodoxy, and a 'Young-Hegelian' view that found tensions in his works and sought to highlight ideas that ran counter to prevailing political and religious doctrine. Hegel's works contained ideas which, so the politically and theologically radical 'Young Hegelians' believed, were more 'dangerous' than Hegel could openly admit. Thinking through these ideas and their implications became a central theme of German philosophy and political debate in the 1830s and 1840s and shaped the intellectual climate in which Marx, Engels and Bakunin, among others, grew up.

Our own position takes up this Young (or 'Left') Hegelian tradition and contends that there are differences between Hegel's earlier and later writings which cannot simply be harmonized. One idea above all displays a decisive shift over the course of Hegel's lifetime – *recognition*. Here the chronology of Hegel's life must briefly be explained. By Hegel's 'earlier' writings, we mean, above all, the works which he wrote at Jena – including the *Phenomenology of Spirit*, completed on the eve of the Battle of Jena in 1806 and published the next year. The 'later' works include the lecture series and volumes – including the *Philosophy of Right* of 1821 – which Hegel produced while a professor at Berlin during an era of political restoration and censorship. Why is the relation between Hegel's earlier and later writings important? Why should there be doubt about whether they say the same thing? The crucial circumstance is that, as the dates imply, the earlier works stand closer in time than do the later to the French Revolution of 1789 – of which Hegel was an ardent supporter. As time passed, so we argue, Hegel – whether voluntarily or under duress – made his peace with a social world that was less than revolutionary. Whereas the *Phenomenology of Spirit* could speak in glowing terms of the 'sunburst' of the French Revolution and the 'new world' it created (Hegel 1977: 7), by the time of the *Philosophy of Right* the 'grey-in-grey' (Hegel 2008: 16) of a constitutional monarchy had become Hegel's favoured polity. The flame of a revolution which swept away state power and put authority and hierarchy radically in question had, for Hegel, dimmed.

Present-day commentators tend to play down the question of a contrast between Hegel's earlier and later works. The idea that Hegel's thought forms a seamless whole has once again become the academic consensus. The reasons for this are not clear. In the 1960s and 1970s, perhaps influenced by Karl Marx's *Economic and Philosophical Manuscripts* (Marx and Engels 1975a: esp. 326–46), it was common for treatments of Hegel to focus on the *Phenomenology* – where, it was agreed, an important discussion of recognition was to be found. In the neoliberal years which followed, Hegel and his relation to Marx slipped from the register of academically respectable topics. The *Phenomenology* itself ceased to count, in academia, as an admired, classic text. Alexandre Kojève's *Introduction to the Reading of Hegel* – undoubtedly the most challenging study of the *Phenomenology* as a text – was abjured in terms that went beyond the norms of usual academic debate (see, for example, Williams 1997: 10–13, 366–71). Instead, academic attention shifted to the *Philosophy of Right* where, as was rightly pointed out, the term 'recognition' was again to be found (see, for example, Honneth 2010). The term 'recognition' was remoulded along the *Philosophy of Right*'s lines and in terms that had nothing to do with the French Revolution and, above all, with Marx. The *Philosophy of Right*'s constitutionalism was taken (as it had been by the Old Hegelians) to be Hegel's greatest legacy. In sum, with the emergence of neoliberalism, Hegel commentary lurched into reaction. The present work seeks to reverse this depressing development. *Revolutionary Recognition* attempts to give not merely Hegel in general but the Hegel of the *Phenomenology* his due.

Recognition in the *Phenomenology*

What does the *Phenomenology* tell us? Hegel's is an undeniably complex and even forbidding book, and not all strands in its argument concern us here.[1] What we attempt in this section is a summary of Hegel's thoughts on recognition that underlines their radical, indeed revolutionary, implications. A good place to begin is to note that in *Phenomenology* chapter IV (on 'Self-Consciousness'), the reader first encounters talk of 'recognition', and does so in a striking setting: a narrative of a 'fight to the death' which, in Hegel's view, establishes a relation of mastery (*Herrschaft*) and slavery (*Knechtschaft*). What exactly occurs in this famous 'master-slave' passage? At this point our discussion of Hegel engages with philosophical themes which a reader may feel are ones of detail but that, it turns out, are essential to the argument that our book wishes to make. We ask for the reader's patience and promise that it will be rewarded. The steps in Hegel's argument can best be understood, we suggest, in the following way.

Two human individuals (or as Hegel calls them, two 'self-consciousnesses') encounter one another in a scenario that exists prior to history and outside of society. When they do, they are simply and solely creatures of monological and instrumental desire: they know nothing whatever of social or dialogical or recognitive existence. Because they are simply and solely creatures of desire, they have no alternative but to fight each other. All more 'polite' courses of action being denied to them, they perceive one another merely as unpredictable threats. Because the threat which they pose to one another is potentially mortal, they have no alternative but to struggle to the death. Each seeks 'the death of the other' (Hegel 1977: 113). Note that the fight referred to by Hegel is not, thus envisaged, a fight *for recognition* but a fight for the other's death. It is, in other words, a fight fought for stakes that concern not recognition but the satisfaction of desire: the desire concerned is desire for survival and the continuation of 'life' (Hegel 1977: 106). As the fight proceeds, one self-consciousness falls into the power of the other. How this happens is incidental to the story; one self-consciousness may slip and tumble and now cowers on the ground as the other raises his or her arm to deliver the death blow. Note that there is nothing in the least mysterious in this – but what happens next is all-important. Having lost advantage, and exposed him- or herself to attack, the self-consciousness who has slipped (and who will presently become slave) experiences 'absolute fear' (Hegel 1977: 117).

Fearfully, the slave-to-be gazes into the triumphant self-consciousness's murderous and death-intending eyes. What the slave-to-be sees in the eyes of the other (the eyes of the self-consciousness who will become master) is nothing but his or her own death – or intended death. It is at this crucial point – we may say, summarizing Hegel's line of thought – that the cowering and defeated self-consciousness cries 'I submit!' With this cry of submission, mastery and slavery come into existence, and the 'one-sided and unequal' recognition (Hegel 1977: 116) that paradigmatically characterizes a master-slave relation is born. It is at this point in Hegel's envisioned scenario that, strictly speaking, the 'master-slave dialectic' begins.

One-sided and unequal recognition as instanced in a master-slave relation is, Hegel tells us, unstable and self-undermining: a master (in order to count as a master, as someone free) depends on recognition by a slave, but the slave himself is, for the master, unworthy of recognition, a mere thing. As unfree, the slave could recognize the master only under duress, rendering that recognition worthless. The slave is, in Hegel's words, too enmeshed in 'thinghood' (1977: 115) to count as one whose recognition has any value. The master requires but can only disparage the slave's recognition. The master could be affirmed as free only by one who is themselves free; something the very relationship of mastery and slavery forbids. The lesson a reader of the *Phenomenology* learns from pondering the 'master-slave dialectic' is that 'one-sided and unequal recognition' is *contradictory*.[2] Domination (*Herrschaft*) of one person by another is not simply morally pernicious but contradicts itself – it *does not* and *cannot* achieve what it seeks. Only where both persons in a relationship are really free and hence give their recognition freely is recognition *mutual* and thus uncontradictory. In Hegel's words, only in a situation where self-consciousnesses 'recognize themselves as mutually recognizing one another' (1977: 112) does recognition exist in an uncontradicted or non-alienated form. The solution to the problem of master and slave is to end domination altogether.

The fight that established mastery and slavery is, in the *Phenomenology*'s argument, the *beginning of history* – history being seen as a succession of patterns of recognition. Yet recognition between a master and slave is, as we have seen, contradictory. It lacks the 'reciprocity' (1977: 111–12) or to-and-fro dynamic that 'pure' or 'mutual' recognition (1977: 112) entails. It is self-defeating. For the *Phenomenology*, it may be said, history is the story of the *overcoming of contradicted or contradictory recognition* and the *bringing into being of mutual recognition*. History thus ends when the slave breaks free of his chains and seizes his autonomy, when (in Hegel's words) he 'destroys this alien negative moment, posits himself as a negative in the permanent order of things, and thereby becomes for himself (*für sich*), someone existing on his own account' (Hegel 1977: 118).[3]

For the Hegel of the *Phenomenology*, we propose, history is a history of recognition. That is to say, it is a history of forms (or patterns) which, over time, recognition takes. Such a history *begins* when recognition comes into existence – or, at least, when recognition becomes an issue which human action may address. Such history *ends* either when recognition vanishes from the face of the earth or (less disastrously) when history's narrative culminates in recognition that is uncontradicted. In the *Phenomenology*, history is a path of 'doubt' and 'despair' (Hegel 1977: 49) that, against expectations, ends in the latter of the aforementioned ways. More, it ends in Hegel's own lifetime, in French Revolutionary years. With the *Phenomenology*, 'philosophy' (or love of wisdom) is raised to the level of 'science' (or actual wisdom), and this is possible because it is written in the light of the French Revolutionary 'sunburst' – a sunburst which illuminates the features of a 'new world' (Hegel 1977: 3–4, 7).[4]

Between the *beginning* and the *end* of Hegelian history, there obtain numerous patterns of contradictory recognition – or 'misrecognition' – and, at the risk of imposing unity on an intrinsically untidy and uncertain process, history is for the *Phenomenology* the process which transforms contradictory recognition into recognition of an uncontradicted (or 'non-alienated') sort. The very first pattern of recognition which exists in history is, for Hegel, the 'one-sided and unequal' recognition characteristic of a master-slave relation (Hegel 1977: 116). But one-sided and unequal recognition is not the only form of recognition which prevails throughout history's course. (We will outline the other historically prevalent form of contradictory recognition presently.)

To the foregoing general observations on recognition and history, comments on the related theme of *freedom* need to be added. This is so because, for Hegel, the notions of recognition and freedom presuppose one another. In the *Phenomenology*'s understanding of history, freedom and recognition are conjoint themes. Freedom – which, for the Hegel of the *Phenomenology*, signifies *self-determination*[5] – subsists through recognition and vice versa: an individual's capacity to determine him- or herself is contradicted unless it is recognized, and recognition is contradicted unless it is free. What this means is that freedom and recognition flourish *only together*. If one of these is impaired or contradicted or alienated, so is the other. When either freedom or recognition comes into its own, and exists on its own terms in a 'non-alienated' fashion, so too must the other. If uncontradicted freedom or uncontradicted recognition is to be possible, a terrain of what the *Phenomenology* terms 'mutual recognition' must obtain.

Standing back, we may map these reflections on to what has been said about the course of history and history's end. This mapping is (a reader may be relieved to learn) extremely straightforward. The picture that, we suggest, a reader needs to hold in mind takes the form of a timeline: throughout the course of history, freedom (understood as self-determination) and recognition are, alike, alienated and contradicted. At the end of history, freedom and recognition flourish together in a mutually recognitive 'new world'. Academic commentaries of recent years often fall silent when it comes to considering the *Phenomenology*'s searching and deeply moving treatment of emancipation. It has become common to think of Hegel as a philosopher of a freedom available only through institutions; above all, the institutions of the state. Yet only the later Hegel says as much; the *Phenomenology* tells us something very different.

If history *begins* with the fight that results in mastery and slavery, it *ends* when mutual or uncontradicted recognition is achieved.[6] For the Hegel of the *Phenomenology*, there is one particular event which brings this history of contradictory recognition to an end: the French Revolution. Only in his description of the revolutionary crowd activity on the streets of Paris (Hegel 1977: 355–63) does Hegel – after 200 pages of historical-philosophical discussion – return to the language of reciprocity and unconstrained interaction he had used when first describing recognition. Mutual recognition, in other words, is the emancipated existence towards which the French Revolution aims.

This has not merely practical import. When the revolution occurs, it is – Hegel tells us – 'time for philosophy [etymologically, love of wisdom] to be raised to the status of a science [actual wisdom]' (1977: 3–4). The 'absolute freedom' witnessed in the revolution and the 'absolute knowing' which crowns the *Phenomenology*'s philosophical development are one.

What do we mean when we say that, throughout history, recognition has existed in a 'contradicted' or alienated fashion? We have already referred to one example of this. Recognition between a master (*Herr*) and a slave (*Knecht*) is *one-sided and unequal*; it lacks a *reciprocity* that is vital to recognition per se. Stated differently, 'one-sided and unequal' recognition does not have the to-and-fro dynamic that mutuality involves. However, *one-sided and unequal* recognition is not, in the *Phenomenology*, the only form that contradictory recognition takes. Here, we note the second form. We do so not merely for reasons of scholarly completeness. The second form is central to our argument and, as we will see in Chapter 2, is taken up by Marx in his critique of the market. Hegel's discussion of contradictory recognition sheds light on the Hegel–Marx relation.

For reasons that will become apparent, we refer to the second form as *institutional recognition*. When Hegel introduces this form, he does so in an oblique and, at first, puzzling way. In the course of a lengthy discussion of social alienation, a reader of the *Phenomenology* encounters the assertion that 'nature displays itself in the universal elements of air, water, fire and earth' (1977: 300). What does Hegel mean here? Has a manuscript on nature been interwoven in Hegel's essentially social text? We suggest a simpler explanation. Hegel is drawing an analogy between a specific form of alienation and existence of a natural kind. The analogy is made explicit when Hegel tells us, a few lines later, that 'spirit' – here he means, in effect, society – 'displays itself in . . . universal – but here spiritual [or social] – "masses or spheres"'

(1977: 300). What, a reader may ask, is a spiritual or social mass? Our reply to this question is that spiritual masses (*geistige Massen*) in Hegel's terminology are *social institutions*. In social institutions, role definitions inhere. Hegel's point is that social institutions pick up traditions and acquire something very like momentum in the natural sense. In the state, for example, one does not simply engage in politics but *becomes 'a politician'*; in universities, one does not simply teach or learn but *becomes 'a lecturer' or 'a student'*. Institutions and the role definitions to which they give rise become a second nature. Yet institutions recognize us in a fundamentally contradictory way.

Hegel's critique of social institutions ('spiritual masses') follows logically from his understanding of recognition. Institutions alienate individuals because – by their very nature – they can only recognize individuals as instances of a general type, and must cast particularities and peculiarities aside. Institutions recognize us, Hannah Arendt notes, 'as such and such, that is, as something which we fundamentally are not' (1975: 13–14). Law and legislation, in their very indiscriminate and general character, are obvious instances of this. But the market, particularly in its capitalist form, is also an institution in which recognition of an abstractly universal sort reigns. There a social division of labour generates forms of recognition similarly abstract in character. That individuals sometimes affirm identities based on this contradictory form of recognition – 'I am a lecturer' or 'I am a student' or 'I am a civil servant' – indicates how deep institutional alienation runs.

Underlying Hegel's critique of institutional recognition is the suggestion that individuals who recognize one another in terms of role definitions recognize or acknowledge one another in an incomplete way. If, for example, individuals recognize one another only *as lecturers* or *as students* or *as proprietors*, and so on, the parts of their being which fall outside of the role definition concerned go without acknowledgement. If, by way of contrast, we think of the eighteenth-century locution 'The whole human being moves together', it becomes clear what is missing when role definitions hold sway. It is obvious too that even if recognition is *reciprocal* it may yet still fail to exist in a humanly rewarding and non-alienated way. Reciprocity is a necessary but not sufficient condition of mutual recognition. What is also necessary is that recognition not be constrained by the acting out of a social or economic role. For the *whole* human being – not just a part – to 'move together', institutions must be cast aside.

Earlier, we suggested that, according to the *Phenomenology*, recognition throughout history is contradictory – in one respect or another. History ends, or reaches its culmination, when mutual or non-alienated recognition is achieved. Marx's 'communism', we will argue in Chapter 2, is heir to this idea of a society of a mutually recognitive kind. Our present task is to make clear what mutual recognition entails. For Hegel, mutual recognition is a space of freedom. In a mutually recognitive society, individuals are free not *in spite of* one another – as is the case where scenarios of 'negative' freedom are upheld (see esp. Berlin 2006) – but *in and through* one another. As Sartre puts it (in a highly Hegelian formulation), our freedom 'depends entirely upon the freedom of others' just as 'the freedom of others depends upon our own' (2007: 48). My freedom is not limited by the presence of an other but is complemented and enriched by it. It is through mutual recognition's fusion of 'independence' and 'dependence' – the keywords of the title Hegel gave the master-slave passage – that the problem of contradictory recognition is solved.

For this to be the case, the term 'recognition' must have not merely a cognitive but a constitutive force. Recognition is *cognitive* when, say, a familiar building is identified as it gradually appears through mist.

Recognition is *constitutive*, by contrast, when it makes the recognized object or person who or what he or she is. In Hegel's words, 'self-consciousness exists in and for itself when, and by the fact that, it so exists for another; that is, it exists only in being recognized [*es ist nur als ein Annerkanntes*]' (1977: 111, translation amended). If recognition is constitutive in this way, the notion of individuals as free in and through one another makes complete sense. Individuals who recognize one another do not sit indifferently alongside one another as externally related entities. On the contrary, they accentuate one another's freedom and throw one another's freedom into relief. This in turn is what allows Hegel to say that 'self-consciousnesses' (i.e. mutually recognitive human individuals) 'in their opposition, enjoy perfect freedom and independence' (1977: 110). To the extent that freedom is constituted through recognition, Hegel may say this with no determinist strings being attached.

When mutual recognition obtains, what, exactly, is recognized? Our answer is, the freedom (the self-determination) of individuals – as many individuals as exist. To use a metaphor that will recur in our book, in a good conversation, each participant is taken to be responsible for his or her utterances. He or she is taken to mean what he or she says. Each participant is *recognized* – which is not to say that his or her views need be endorsed. The validity of the participant's claim is not constituted or endorsed by recognition but the self-determination and 'independence' (Hegel) of the participant is. The same applies not only to conversation but, for example, also to political action. In a situation of mutual recognition, each individual's political acts are recognized as those of a self-determining being. If their acts are suppressed or denied then mutual recognition falls back into contradictory recognition, just as a conversation which merely follows the dictates or norms of an institutional role ceases to be 'good' conversation.

A number of other implications follow from Hegel's understanding of mutual recognition. First, Hegel does not say that what is recognized is my identity, or my status, or my prestige, or my rights. He does not presuppose any human qualities or attributes already present that are 'worthy' of being recognized. In Chapter 3 we will see that this misunderstanding of recognition is sadly widespread in the academic discourse of recognition. It is a misunderstanding that makes of recognition the moral desideratum of *respect*. Recognition in Hegel's view is wholly different from respect. Notions of respect assume the very respect-worthy human qualities or actions they are to prove; they are question-begging. Well aware of the dangers of circularity, Hegel's *Phenomenology* takes nothing for granted in philosophical terms and in particular nothing about human being. What defines humans, according to Hegel, is that they are *not defined*: they are self-defining, self-determining or better – they mutually define each other through their interaction, through the very act of recognition itself. If what is recognized is self-determination, then it is a self-determination incompatible with any pre-given qualities, any status, any identity.

Second, the fluidity of freedom in Hegel's *Phenomenology* is to be emphasized. If history is a sequence of patterns of recognition, and if recognition (in order to count as such) must be freely given, history does not have a pre-established course. For the Hegel of the *Phenomenology*, it *so happens* that history has ended, but there is nothing – no fixed human nature or quasi-natural momentum – that guides history to this outcome. History in the *Phenomenology* is not orchestrated by a demiurge. No 'cunning of reason' operates. There is no question, in Hegel, of a fixed-and-given human nature coming into its own. History – or 'prehistory' (see Marx 1971: 22) – may end in the sense that we have stipulated but there is no question of a 'grand totalizer' – we borrow Sartre's expression (see 2004: 64) – pulling history's strings.

Third, and following from this, for human beings (or self-consciousnesses) to be free through mutually recognitive relations, mutual recognition must be unstructured. In proposing that mutual recognition is unstructured, we do not propose that it is a matter of random chance. What we mean is that mutually recognitive interaction gives the law to itself – just as a good conversation follows its subject matter wherever the subject matter leads. If mutually recognitive interaction becomes dictated by powerful individuals or channelled into the requirements of this or that social institution, then recognition of a contradictory sort is in play. If there is a 'tragic' side to recognition it is that only the participants can prevent this slide into contradictory recognition from occurring.

Let us return to the event with which, we have suggested, the *Phenomenology*'s history ends. Earlier, we suggested that, according to Hegel, mutual recognition makes its appearance when the French Revolution takes place. Yet the section of the book which is devoted to the revolution ('Absolute Freedom and Terror' – 1977: 355–63) is far from triumphalist or celebratory in tone. It is one of the work's darkest passages. What is going on? Is Hegel's message the traditional pessimistic one that the French Revolution 'devours its children'? Does he tell us that a freedom that is unlimited leads inevitably to self-destruction? Nothing in Hegel's discussion, we argue, allows such a conclusion to be drawn. Any understanding of the passage must give not only 'Terror' but also 'Absolute Freedom' its due.

Central to Hegel's account of the French Revolution is the insurgent crowd activity of 1789 (of which the storming of the Bastille is the most famous moment). In this crowd activity, Hegel tells us, 'self-consciousness . . . grasps the fact that its certainty of itself is the essence of all the spiritual "masses", or spheres, of the real as well as the supersensible world' (1977: 356). The social and religious institutions of the *ancien régime* are recognized by the revolutionaries as their own alienated doing, their own estranged will. Now casting off the 'empty thought' of 'silent assent', or 'assent by a representative', the revolutionaries withdraw their acquiescence to oppression and become 'a real general will, the will of all individuals as such' (1977: 357). They tear down the structures that have dominated them.[7] The core of the revolution, Hegel argues, is an insurgent crowd which *puts mutually recognitive freedom into practice*. In its actions, each individual 'always does everything' and 'what appears as done by the whole' is 'the direct and conscious deed of each' (1977: 357).[8] The mutual recognition that was glimpsed at the beginning of history reappears finally – and gloriously – at its end. The radical message of Hegel's discussion of the French Revolution is nothing less than an image of *revolutionary grassroots activity as mutual recognition*.

So far, so good. In the revolution, mutual recognition is an actuality. History has ended. What happens next? An emancipation that exists in and through crowd activity is evanescent – as Hegel knows very well. What happens is that the revolutionaries try to give mutual recognition and revolutionary freedom *stability*. They try to give mutual recognition social instantiation – without which it would remain a protest and an uprising but not the everyday life of freedom. The difficulty is that the steps that the revolutionaries take to preserve freedom undermine freedom itself. A *serial* group (to borrow Sartre's terminology in his *Critique of Dialectical Reason*) lacks the spontaneity and elan of an insurrectionary *group-in-fusion*. As the 'Absolute Freedom and Terror' section of the *Phenomenology* explains, the French Revolution undermines itself. The 'universal work' of drafting a constitution becomes the revolutionaries' first 'task' (Hegel 1977: 357). But a constitution which, for example, distinguishes legislature and executive is a static structure which stands over against the fluidity that freedom entails; it is an 'abstraction'

(Hegel 1977: 359) from freedom itself. For this reason, attempts at constitution-building fail and factionalism takes hold (Hegel 1977: 360). Factionalism not only contradicts the general will but also allows hierarchy (i.e. contradictory recognition) to re-emerge. Robespierre comes to power and institutes a 'Law of Suspects' in which being suspected of betraying the Republic 'has the significance and effect of being guilty' (Hegel 1977: 360). The revolution becomes a state-led 'fury of destruction' (Hegel 1977: 359): the guillotine which had dethroned the absolute monarch now puts another absolute power in his place. Not even the revolutionary *sans-culottes* are safe from the 'unmediated . . . negation' of the terror where the 'sole work and deed' was '*death*' (Hegel 1977: 360, emphasis in original). This is the beginning of the end of revolutionary hopes. Individuals, says Hegel, who have 'felt the fear of death' readily 'return to an apportioned and limited task', 'arrange themselves' once more 'under the various spheres (*Massen*)' (1977: 361) and the revolution as an active and mutually recognitive process is over.

Nothing in the revolution's dissipation was necessary, however; the failure lay in the form in which revolutionaries sought to sustain their freedom. Mutual recognition emerged in Paris but did not achieve social instantiation. History ended – briefly – only for hierarchy and alienation to appear once again. The problem Hegel identifies is this: mutual recognition *cannot* be institutionalized. As attempts at constitution-building were forced to acknowledge, a freedom that is institutionalized contradicts itself.

Hegel knows all this when he writes the *Phenomenology*. He knows, when he is addressing a 'public', which he took to be mutually recognitive, that he is clutching at straws. The *Phenomenology* – Hegel's greatest and most challenging book – is a raw and ragged and counterfactual text. Precisely because it is raw, it could form the starting point for Left-Hegelian or Young-Hegelian discussion.[9] Edgar Bauer's 'free community'

(Stepelevich 1983: 273), Max Stirner's 'Association of Egoists' and – not least – Marx's communist society where 'the free development of each is the condition for the free development of all' (Marx and Engels 1976b: 506) are each attempts to realize the mutual recognition which slipped from the French Revolution's hands. For the Young Hegelians, as for Marx, the attempt to give freedom social instantiation remains an unfinished task. Courageously, Hegel leaves the *Phenomenology* with an inharmonious ending. 'Left' and 'Young' Hegelianism – and Marx – grapple with the revolutionary issues that the *Phenomenology* raised.

Recognition in Hegel's later work

In neoliberal times a distinctive interpretation of Hegel has emerged.[10] It is one where a notion of recognition has developed that is indebted not so much to Hegel's *Phenomenology* but to his later *Philosophy of Right*, a text of which Marx, famously, was highly critical (Marx and Engels 1975a: 5–29).

Does it make sense (a reader of Hegel may ask) to see a continuity between Hegel's use of 'recognition' in his early work and in his *Philosophy of Right*? Can recognition be regarded as a theme that retained its meaning for Hegel throughout his life? Our initial reaction to these questions is to hesitate: an answer depends on the sense in which the term 'recognition' is understood. What is undeniable is that the term is still used by Hegel on a number of occasions in the *Philosophy of Right* (see, for example, 2008: 133, 178, 197, 226, 235), although the nuances he gives it are not always clear. Our reaction becomes less hesitant when the question is sharpened. If it is asked whether recognition in the sense used in the *Philosophy of Right* is the same as that used in the *Phenomenology of Spirit*, our answer is a decided No.

From the standpoint of Hegel's *Phenomenology*, the use of recognition in the *Philosophy of Right* must appear problematic. This is so for several reasons. The first of these concerns the overall architectonic of the later work. The *Philosophy of Right* divides a polity which – Hegel asserts – has the character of 'freedom made actual' (2008: 26) into three 'spheres'. These spheres are *the family, civil society* and *state* (2008: 50–1). The very fact that here free social existence is divided up into spheres or powers entails, we suggest, that the recognition that obtains there is constrained. It is constrained by the very existence of institutions which, for all their potentially benign character, can only stand over against the individual. In the introductory paragraphs of its 'Ethical Life' section, the *Philosophy of Right* tells its reader that 'ethical substance and its laws and powers are on the one hand an object [*Gegenstand*]. . . . On the other hand, they are not something alien to the subject' (2008: 155). If the insights of the *Phenomenology* into the alienated and contradictory character of institutional recognition are borne in mind, then this 'on the one hand'/'on the other' formulation is without conceptual foundation. Hegel is trying to square a circle. A social reality of which the *Philosophy of Right* approves stands over against an individual subject, and spiritual masses – however rightful[11] – continue their alienating rule.

Second, specific passages in the *Philosophy of Right* suggest to us that the later Hegel took particular institutions for granted in ways which the Hegel of the *Phenomenology* had not. Where forms of contradictory recognition were uncovered and critiqued in the earlier work, in the later work they receive ethical and legal justification. An example can serve as illustration. Hegel's discussion of property, which forms a core part of his exposition of freedom in the early part of the *Philosophy of Right*, seems to us to forget the recognitive insights of the earlier work. The *Philosophy of Right* calls property 'the primary mode of freedom'

(2008: 52). 'In his property', writes Hegel, 'a person exists for the first time as reason' (2008: 58).[12] Property is in turn 'realized' in law and its infringement (theft) becomes a justified ground for punishment. The Hegel of the *Philosophy of Right* will go even further: the punishment of acts such as theft is the *fulfilment of the criminal's own deed*: 'The injury which falls on the criminal is not merely just *in itself* – as just, it is *eo ipso* his will as it is in itself, an existence of his freedom, *his* right – but it is also a right *posited in the criminal himself*, i.e. in his objectively existent will, in his action' (2008: 102, emphasis in original). Further such examples of the *Philosophy of Right*'s justification of institutions could be given, but a reader begins to see what has changed. Institutions that bear the mark of domination – above all, penal law – are viewed by the late Hegel as manifestations of freedom and are to be recognized by the individual as such. The logical justification Hegel gives them jars uncomfortably with what we had learned of recognitive freedom from the *Phenomenology*. A troubling apologia is given to unfreedoms which the young Hegel would surely not have countenanced.[13]

Defenders of the late Hegel (or of a 'systematic' Hegel) often have a response ready to our line of argument. That response is to argue that a baseline of negative freedoms and rights is always protected in the *Philosophy of Right*; these are to be understood as *sublated* (in the sense of the German word *aufgehoben*: preserved yet superseded) in the higher freedom embodied in the state. The Hegelian state outlaws tyranny by preserving the very liberal freedoms which it deepens in the form of social freedom. The institutions of the state come to *embody freedom* – so runs this response. Does the notion of institutions which *embody freedom* undermine our claims? Our reply is a sceptical one. An institution which *embodies* anything still stands over against the individual: no institution, by very definition, is capable of recognizing an individual's freedom in its full breadth and depth. The freedom which an institution claims to embody can only ever be a freedom that is limited rather than absolute.

A defender of the *Philosophy of Right* faces a further difficulty. If he or she maintains that the state 'embodies' freedom, they are forced to address the thorny problem of how that state is to be harmonized with the second crucial sphere of Hegel's triad, *civil society* (*bürgerliche Gesellschaft*), by which he means, in effect, the market economy. In his early work Hegel had seen civil society as a realm of generalized egoism, a 'monstrous system' which 'moves about blindly, like the elements', and requires continual 'taming like a wild beast' (1979: 249). If civil society – as even the late Hegel admits – is characterized by vast disparities of wealth, by '[w]rongs done to one class by another', where a 'rabble of paupers' is driven to 'inner indignation against the rich, against society, against the government, etc.' (1979: 221), then how can this sphere be controlled except in haphazard and amelioristic ways? If the state is constantly having to tame the market 'monster', then in what sense can we call such a polity – as Hegel does – 'rational'?[14]

Why (a reader of our discussion may wonder) does it greatly matter whether the notion of recognition remains a constant in Hegel's early and later work? Are our comments on the *Philosophy of Right* of interest only in a scholarly sense? In order to provide a sense of why an interpretation of the *Philosophy of Right* is important, we reverse the terms of our initial question. Instead of asking whether recognition is the key which unlocks the *Philosophy of Right*, we ask whether the *Philosophy of Right* supplies a criterion by which the notion of recognition may be measured. And we suggest that drawing one's notion of recognition from the *Philosophy of Right* shifts this notion on to less-than-revolutionary ground. Note that our evident suspicion of the *Philosophy of Right* is not based on a suggestion that the later Hegel is a died-in-the-wool conservative. On the contrary, we are here in sympathy with the 'consensus of contemporary scholarship', as Beiser describes it, 'The consensus of contemporary scholarship is that Hegel was a liberal reformer, and the reactionary interpretation has now been so discredited that it has virtually attained the status of a myth' (Beiser 2005: 216–17; 222–3). Our worry is that the standpoint of a 'liberal reformer' itself makes its peace with an alienated world and contains a conformist tinge.

In the previous section we exhibited Hegel – or, more precisely, the Hegel of the *Phenomenology* – as a theorist whose work on recognition is revolutionary rather than merely liberal and institution-oriented. Although recent academic literature on recognition admits that the *Phenomenology* is a classic of the genre, when one sets Hegel's text of 1806–7 alongside this literature it is clear that much has changed. Most dramatically, in the recent literature the entire critique of what we have termed 'institutional recognition' has dropped out of consideration. And the cost of its dropping out of consideration is that theories of recognition take their bearing from a still-alienated world. It is far from accidental, we suggest, that the Hegel that Axel Honneth (who we discuss in Chapter 3) refers to most frequently is the Hegel not of the *Phenomenology* but of the *Philosophy of Right*.

If the *Phenomenology* still breathes the air of the revolution, by the time of the *Philosophy of Right* and his professorship at the University of Berlin, Hegel no longer writes and thinks explicitly in revolutionary terms.[15] For the *Phenomenology*, mutual recognition was a 'new world' which a revolution might attain. For the *Philosophy of Right*, the only form of recognition on offer is structured by institutions of the post-revolutionary world and the role definitions these afford: family, civil society and the state. Honneth, who patterns his own discussion on the *Philosophy of Right*'s ethical spheres, allows that Hegel's tripartite distinction is marked by 'conservatism' (Honneth 2016: 173), yet the same triad of spheres – given new names – still forms the insuperable horizon of his own political vision.

What is lacking in Hegel's later writings and in present-day commentators on Hegel, and what was present in the *Phenomenology*, is a sense of the depth that the distinction between contradicted and uncontradicted recognition may reach.[16] What is lacking in current debates on recognition is the *Phenomenology*'s insight that freedom points – in revolutionary ways – beyond institutions, hierarchies, role definitions and the division of society into spheres. This is what is so *dangerous* in Hegel's idea.

Revolutionary recognition

At the core of our book is the notion of recognition as a space of unconstrained freedom, as a *revolutionary* phenomenon. In what sense is mutual recognition revolutionary? Our answer does not rely solely on the *Phenomenology*'s favourable comments on the French Revolution but on the radical implications of the 'master-slave' passage which we have also brought to light. Only a recognition that *eschews domination and rejects institutions* is – according to the conditions Hegel's sets himself in the *Phenomenology* – recognition of a non-contradictory sort. We freely admit that, among Hegel scholarship, this is an unorthodox view. Just as readily do we acknowledge that in championing the early against the later Hegel, we commit what for some Hegel scholars is sacrilege: we reject the assumption that his work forms an unbroken whole. Yet in arguing this we can call upon precedent: the Left-Hegelian tradition which saw inconsistencies and lacunae in Hegel's work has produced the most productive reading of Hegel to date; it is no coincidence that Left Hegelianism and revolution are closely linked.

We have discussed Hegel's *Phenomenology of Spirit* in an all-too brief and schematic fashion. We have focused on lines of thought that, especially in neoliberal years, commentators on Hegel have tended to ignore. We close this chapter by accentuating three such strands that a reader should take from the *Phenomenology*.

First, we emphasize that mutually recognitive freedom is freedom of an unstructured kind. If recognition is to be uncontradicted, it can only be unstructured – not in the sense that it is chaotic but in the sense that it follows its own dynamic. (In the same sense, a good conversation must follow its subject matter wherever this subject matter leads.) Mutual recognition must be informal or, to put the point differently, unconstrained and uncoerced. It must be unconstrained by imbalances of power or by institutions which require it to follow this or that formally prescribed course. Mutual recognition is the form of practice which exists in unity with scientific theory because there and there alone conversation is 'good', conversation and interaction prioritizes truth. When it allows itself to be channelled by this or that extraneous institution or norm, conversation ceases to be 'rigorous' or 'good'. The same is the case where political action is concerned. Mutual recognition continues in being when, and only when, it consults itself in unconstrained manner. If political action is guided by leaders or representatives or by this or that institution (or 'spiritual mass'), the to-and-fro dynamic of mutuality evaporates, and emancipation is no longer in play.

Second, we acknowledge a reader's inevitable worry that the conditions we attach to mutual recognition are too stringent. Have we presented a vision of interaction that is idyllic and unrealistic? In answering this misgiving, we point the reader to a passage in the *Phenomenology* where mutual recognition is portrayed in far from idyllic terms. When mutual recognition exists, Hegel says, an action

– any action – is 'placed' before others. It is performed in the knowledge that others will interpret it. So far so good. But, says Hegel, what is 'placed [*hinstellt*]' is also 'displaced [*verstellt*]' (1977: 394). It may be misinterpreted or involve dissemblance. Stated differently, *possibilities of acting in bad faith* continue, even where mutual recognition is in play. Indeed, possibilities of acting in bad faith increase – or become more of an issue. When individuals act in terms of role definitions it is, strictly speaking, *irrelevant* what 'private' attitude an individual adopts towards his or her performance. If, say, a 'lecturer' lectures, students need not ask questions about his or her attitude to academic life. When, by contrast, a mutually recognitive individual 'places' a speech or action before others, and asks for it to be acknowledged, *it matters* whether the speech or action is performed in good faith. In Hegel's view, there are ways inherent to mutual recognition that mean free interaction can go off the rails. It does *not* follow from this, we add, that mutual recognition is *inexorably trapped* in bad faith or misrecognition – as Lacan's influential misreading of Hegel has it.[17] What *does* follow is that mutual recognition exists only while it renews itself. No natural momentum propels society towards mutual recognition or can hold society to it once it is achieved. The cost of mutual recognition is that it must continually be re-projected. Whenever it is taken for granted, contradictory recognition is waiting in the wings.

Third, we emphasize once more the revolutionary implications of Hegel's notion of recognition: his is *a critique of all forms of domination*. Seeing this has often been difficult for a reader of Hegel because the terms which underline it are often lost in English translation. An English reader who sees the words 'master' and 'slave' may assume Hegel is criticizing long-gone feudal relations; slavery, where it exists today, is often viewed as 'anachronistic'. But Hegel's German terms *Herrschaft* (mastery, domination) and *Knechtschaft* (slavery, subjugation) carry no historically specific connotations; they can occur at any time or in any place. This helps explain why Marx would take up Hegel's term *Herrschaft* to describe capital's rule (see Chapter 2). And just as Hegel's critique of domination could appeal to Marx, so it could appeal in the twentieth century to such radical thinkers as Simone de Beauvoir and Frantz Fanon.[18] These thinkers confirm Hegel's argument that whenever domination appears, it not only is morally deplorable but also contradicts itself – it rests on shaky ground. The earthquake of radical thought set in motion by Hegel rumbles on long after his death, sometimes dormant, sometimes active. It is time, we believe, to make it active again.

We mention one such 'aftershock' of Hegelian radicalism here: the work of Guy Debord. Debord notes that 'all the theoretical currents of the revolutionary working-class movement – Stirner and Bakunin as well as Marx – grew out of a critical confrontation with Hegelian thought' (1987: 39). If we understand 'critical' to mean not just oppositional but taking Hegel seriously, then Debord is surely right. Interestingly, Debord expresses his famous notion of the 'spectacle' – the extreme alienation of the present day – in recognitive terms. The spectacle, he says,

> systematically destroys the 'faculty of encounter' and replaces it with a *social hallucination*: a false consciousness of encounter, an 'illusion of encounter'. In a society where no one can any longer be *recognized* by others [emphasis in original], each individual becomes incapable of recognizing his own reality. Ideology is at home; separation has built its own world. . . . Imprisoned in a flattened universe bounded by the *screen* of the spectacle that has enthralled him, the spectator knows no one but the fictitious speakers who subject him to a one-way monologue about their commodities and the politics of their commodities. The spectacle as a whole serves as his looking glass. What he sees there are dramatisations of illusory escapes from a universal autism. (1987: 118)

Debord, like Stirner and Bakunin, is an anarchist. What in Hegel's work could possibly give an anarchist inspiration? If Hegel is the thinker of the *Philosophy of Right*, then it seems – very little. But if – as Debord's quote hints – we foreground recognition in its unconstrained *Phenomenology* sense, then we can see why a thoroughgoing anarchist and communist politics might find in Hegel such rich resources.

Mutual recognition, as Debord and others saw, is the solution to the monological alienation of the present world. With this insight, Debord stretches back to shake hands with Hegel's early readers who sensed the revolutionary potential of his thinking. In the years following Hegel's death it was the Young Hegelians – David Friedrich Strauss, Bruno and Edgar Bauer, Moses Hess, Stirner and the young Marx – who renewed his dangerous idea in and against a bourgeois and institutionalized social world. Marx, it is true, is famous as a critic of the Young Hegelians. But it would be more accurate to say that he kept the notion of Hegelian radicalism alive.

2
Marx as thinker of recognition

Just as recognition is at the core of Hegel's thought, so it is at the heart of Marx's thinking and makes sense of a diverse range of Marx's concerns. Of course, to argue that Marx is a thinker of recognition is, in Marxist terms, unorthodox. Due to long-standing prejudices, the concept of recognition has an 'unMarxist' ring. At best, recognition features at the edges of discussion of the topic of alienation; at worst, it is assumed to belong to the Hegelian baggage supposedly jettisoned by the 'mature' Marx. A further prejudice blocks the way to a recognitive reading of Marx, namely the tendency to view his relationship to Hegel through the lens of the 'Critique of the *Philosophy of Right*' (Marx and Engels 1975a: 3–129) and thus to overlook the influence of Hegel's earlier and – as we have argued – more radical *Phenomenology of Spirit*. We suggest that while Marx had justifiable criticisms of the *Philosophy of Right*, his critical attitude did not extend to Hegel's works as a whole. Indeed, his critique of the late Hegel draws upon the very revolutionary resources of the early Hegel, in particular the *Phenomenology*'s notion of recognition. Hegel's and Marx's views of recognition run parallel and, rather than 'turning him on his head', Marx remained a Hegelian throughout his life.

A reader who has an image of recognition as a 'bourgeois' category must therefore set aside their preconceptions when encountering Marx's writings. Marx's view is much more subtle. Recognition is indeed a category upon which bourgeois thinkers and other apologists for capitalism have called, but when understood consistently it is a category which explodes the bourgeois world view. Marx, we believe, takes up Hegel's challenge to expose the contradictory patterns of recognition of his day and to conceive a mutually recognitive existence that would solve these contradictions.

In this chapter we explore a selection of Marx's most relevant texts. Our discussion focuses on three topics which preoccupied Marx throughout his lifetime – commodity exchange, property and class. Through the lens of recognition, we argue, the revolutionary nature of Marx's treatment of these topics becomes clear. These topics are chosen to illustrate what we regard as a fundamental claim: for Marx, recognition is not merely an 'ideological' phenomenon but is equally a 'material' and 'practical' one. Our choice of topics is not to be regarded as partial, though: for us there is *nothing* in Marx which does not turn on recognition (by which we understand 'recognition' in the *Phenomenology*'s sense). The chapter closes with a discussion of communism, which we argue can best be understood by reference to Hegelian mutual recognition. In interpreting communism in these terms we underline Marx's revolutionary vision.

Marx on commodity exchange

A key pillar of political economy – the forebear of today's neoliberal ideology – is the idea that capitalism involves the free exchange of commodities between individuals. One of Marx's greatest insights is to show that this idea rests on a specific – and problematic – manifestation of recognition. In the *Grundrisse* (written 1857–8), Marx points out that for commodity exchange to take place individuals who exchange must first 'mutually recognize one another as proprietors' (1973: 243, translation amended). By this he means that they must first recognize each other as legally free and as the 'rightful' owners of property and agree that 'no one seizes hold of another's property by force. Each divests himself of his property voluntarily' (1973: 243). For Marx, in other words, a key pillar of the capitalist market rests on a recognitive foundation. Yet it is a problematic foundation, as Marx is quick to point out: the recognition that occurs between proprietors is that of the merely formal-legal freedom and equality. Such formal-legal recognition, Marx says, is mere *semblance*: a 'surface process, beneath which, however, in the depths, entirely different processes go on, in which this apparent individual equality and liberty disappear' (1973: 247). Once we take up Marx's invitation to go behind the facade of capitalism as a marketplace where individuals exchange goods on free and equal terms, when we look instead at *capital* and *labour* (which Marx calls the 'prerequisite' of exchange), then this 'equality and freedom . . . prove to be inequality and unfreedom' (1973: 248–9).

That the free exchange of commodities hides a systematic unfreedom is a theme that unites Marx's early and late work. It comes to the fore early on, for instance, in a fascinating discussion of the phenomenon of debt in an article he wrote in 1844. In these so-called *Comments on James Mill* (Marx 1992: 259–78), Marx shows in striking ways how capitalism generates an illusion of mutual recognition that masks a diabolical reality of unfreedom and dependence. The *Comments on James Mill* are relatively unknown to readers of Marx but deserve a place alongside his most famous works. What particularly strikes a reader of this brief but far-reaching text is how closely the language of Marx's discussion of creditor and debtor resembles that of Hegel's treatment of master and slave. The relation of creditor to debtor displays exactly the same contradictory mix of 'independence' (*Selbständigkeit*) and 'dependence' (*Unselbstständigkeit*) which are central to Hegel's discussion. As with the Hegelian master and slave, each of the poles of the creditor–debtor relation is an individual whose being is determined by that relation. What Marx calls the 'bond' of debt defines the identities of the participants, particularly that of the debtor.

> The man in need of credit is not only defined simply by his poverty but also has to put up with the demoralizing judgement that he does not inspire confidence, that he is unworthy of recognition [*Anerkennung*], that he is in short, a social pariah and a bad man. So that in addition to his actual deprivation he has to endure the ignominy of having to ask the rich man for credit. (Marx 1992: 264)[1]

The totality of the poor man's 'social virtues', Marx notes, 'his very existence represent the repayment of his capital together with the usual interest' (Marx 1992: 263). For the creditor, therefore, the death of the debtor (or, we may add, his default) 'is the very worst thing that can happen' (Marx 1992). 'It is self-evident', Marx adds, 'that over and above these moral guarantees the creditor also has the guarantee provided by the force of law' (Marx 1992).

Clearly, recognition is here one-sided and unequal. When it claims to be otherwise it is, Marx says, mere 'dissimulation, hypocrisy and sanctimoniousness' (Marx 1992). The complementing of an individual's freedom that mutual recognition involves has in the credit relationship become 'plunder' and a 'mutual servitude' (*wechselseitige Knechtschaft*) to money. The hypocrisy lies above all in the pretence that this contradictory recognition is the epitome of freedom and equality, that it is 'the greatest possible recognition of man' (Marx 1992: 264). In this world of the 'illusory' mutual recognition presented by political economists such as Mill, we go through the looking glass into a world where human dependence appears as independence and humiliation as dignity. The free market celebrated by the political economist (today we would say – by neoliberal thinkers) is in reality a world where individuality and morality have become 'counterfeited' and 'man himself transformed into money' (Marx 1992: 264). In the topsy-turvy ideas of political economy, contradictory recognition masquerades as mutual recognition.

A world of contradictory recognition, Marx suggests, is *inverted*: everything is the opposite of what it seems. If this is the case, then our picture of Marx's thinking alters: he does not turn Hegel (who is supposedly 'standing on his head') – the right way up. Rather, he works with the same notion of an 'inverted world' (*verkehrte Welt*) of contradictory recognition that Hegel had depicted (see Hegel 1977: 97–8).[2] That contradictory recognition creates such an inverted world can be seen in the numerous references in the *Comments on James Mill* to the 'semblance' (*Schein*) of mutual trust and mutual recognition in the relation between creditor and debtor (see, for example, Marx 1992: 263). Following Hegel, Marx realizes that where contradictory recognition prevails, morality necessarily appears in hypocritical guise. It is with reason that bourgeois morality hides its own essence. The creditor–debtor relation can only appear as mutual recognition in a world where everything is upside down.

The *Comments on James Mill* deal primarily with the credit system and banking, but they hint that contradictory recognition has wider ramifications: that it is a feature of commodity exchange as such. In his later works Marx makes the point explicit. In *Capital*, for instance, he writes that in order for commodities to be exchanged,

> their guardians must place themselves in relation to one another, as persons whose will resides in those objects, and must behave in such

a way that each does not appropriate the commodity of the other, and part with his own, except by means of an act done by mutual consent. They must, therefore, mutually recognise in each other the rights of private proprietors. (Marx 1976: 178, translation amended)

One of the key steps in *Capital* is to show that the hidden presupposition of free commodity exchange is a realm of production where one class (labour) is systematically exploited by another (capital). In other words, behind a relation of apparent recognitive equality lies a relation of recognitive inequality; behind capitalism's appearance of mutual recognition lies contradictory recognition. With that decisive step Marx's great work takes us beyond political economy – with its focus on the realm of exchange, 'where everything takes place on the surface' and where 'liberty, equality, property and Bentham' (1976: 280) are the watchwords – into the 'hidden abode of production', where social relations take a very different form:

> When we leave this sphere of simple circulation or the exchange of commodities, which furnishes the 'free-trader vulgaris' with his views, his concepts and the standard by which he judges the society of capital and wage-labour, a certain change takes place, or so it appears, in the physiognomy of our dramatis personae. He who was previously the money-owner now strides in front as capitalist; the possessor of labour-power follows as his labourer. The one smirks self-importantly and is intent on business; the other is timid and holds back, like one who has brought his own hide to market and now has nothing to expect but – a tanning. (1976: 280)

As with the credit system, freedom for one in the sphere of exchange is unfreedom for another. Both spheres presents the semblance of mutual recognition between 'persons' behind which lies a diabolical reality: the actuality of exploitation – that is, contradictory recognition. Capitalist exploitation, Marx says, is 'veiled slavery' (1976: 925). What capitalism veils, we can now see, is domination (*Herrschaft*) in Hegel's sense.[3]

Exploitation – of worker by capitalist – is an instance of Hegelian *one-sided and unequal recognition*. But, we suggest further, capitalism also involves the *second* form of Hegelian contradictory recognition: *institutional recognition*. In what sense? Capitalist and labourer, Marx's later works tell us, are 'personifications', 'embodiments' or 'incarnations' or 'bearers' (he tries out various metaphors) of particular class relations and interests (1976: 92). The capitalist *just is* capital personified, only as such does he become 'respectable' (1976: 739); the worker *just is* labour personified – lacking means of production, owning only the capacity to work, he or she has become wholly fungible: 'abstract labour' (1976: 159, 989). Both capitalist and worker, Marx says, are thus 'machines' or 'cogs' in a 'social mechanism' (1976: 742, 739) – their roles following inevitably from the institution of the capitalist market. To be labour- or capital-personified is to be an abstraction, all of one's individual characteristics bracketed out and one's many-sidedness reduced to a single generalization. It is, in Marx's striking language (1975: 100, 591, 635), to wear a 'character mask' (*Charaktermaske*).

If capitalism involves not just *one-sided and unequal recognition* but also *institutional recognition*, then crucial implications follow. One is that Marx cannot simply be siding with the category of labour. A class is a pole of a one-sided and unequal recognitive relation. It involves, moreover, role definitions: to be a 'worker', to be a 'member' of the 'working class', is to be recognized in a contradictory way. Such a recognitive identity is not something to be celebrated but something – if possible – to be refused. Could Marx really have believed this? We maintain that he did. Indeed, only if he did believe this can we make sense of the contrast he makes in the *Comments on James Mill* between 'life' and 'labour' (1992: 278), his comments in the *1844 Manuscripts* that 'labour itself . . . is harmful and pernicious' (Marx and Engels 1975a: 240) and his contention in *The German Ideology* that 'communist revolution ... does away with labour' (Marx and Engels 1976a: 52).[4] Finally, only in this light can we make sense of Marx's portrayal of communism in the later writings as a wholly new 'self-conscious activity ... the development of the rich individuality which is all-sided in its production as in its consumption, and whose labour also therefore appears no longer as labour, but as the full development of activity itself' (1973: 325).[5]

A reader unaware of the recognitive theme running through Marx's work can easily be lead astray and seek his view of social 'reality' (as opposed to mere 'semblance') in the realm of production. On the contrary, as *Capital* indicates, individuals in the realm of production still wear masks ('personae' in its original Greek meaning) and 'personification' remains a guise. Just as capitalism appears as voluntary exchange between contracting 'persons', so 'worker' and 'capitalist' are not just classes but abstractions which misrecognize (and thus alienate) the individuals concerned.[6] By implication – and the point is far-reaching – such abstractions are incompatible with an emancipated world. Communism, as Marx conceives it, is not a reversal in the hierarchy of capitalist and worker but the detonation of both roles. It is in this – faithfully Marxist – sense that Ernst Bloch writes,

> every kind of *Proletkult* is false, and a bourgeois infection. It purports to provide the key to the larder of humanity, yet cannot claim to carry, let alone to be, this larder. In its dehumanization it teaches, with radical precision, that there has never yet been human life, but only ever economic life, which drives humans about, making them false. (2006: 18, translation amended)

At the start of this section we mentioned the need to discard a prejudice – that recognition is a bourgeois ideal. Have we justified our case for recognition being a revolutionary rather than an affirmative category? Does Marx really adopt mutual recognition as a guiding principle or does he simply expose its hypocritical use by political economy? Our response is that the two possibilities are not exclusive. When Marx criticizes 'political economic recognition' – that between creditor and debtor or that between owners of commodities – he is implicitly opposing to it a form of recognition that would be more than merely formal, illusory and hypocritical. Marx is a critic not of recognition but of the semblance of mutual recognition where its opposite prevails. His works – and here no break between 'young' and 'mature' Marx is to be found – expose the reversal of equality and freedom into their opposite, of mutual recognition into contradictory recognition. To criticize this inversion – as Marx does – is implicitly to uphold mutual recognition as one's principle. Only from such a standpoint – a proleptic standpoint, a standpoint of emancipation – can one so criticize. Mutual recognition becomes for Marx (as it was for Hegel) the measure by which its own reversal into contradictory recognition can be judged. Marx's critique rests upon no other values than the mutual recognition that capitalism in its very essence undermines.[7]

Marx on property

A very general but, at the same time, telling observation sets the scene to our discussion of property: in both his early and his later writings, Marx thinks of property not as an object but in terms of relations between human individuals. This understanding of property in terms of social relations deserves emphasis and, before embarking on textual discussion, we offer three comments. First, a discussion of property *in terms of social relations* is far from uncontroversial. For example, property is seen in liberal political theory as something – some *object* – which may be owned individually, or distributed or carved up. A difficulty with thinking of property *as an object* is that it is, so to say, a 'social' rather than a 'natural' object: to think of property as an object is to picture it as something which may be used and owned in this or that socially specific way. Second, if property is viewed not *as an object* but *in terms of social relations*, an evident question arises as to how relations between individuals are to be seen. Our proposal is that social relations are to be seen as *relations of recognition* – whether contradictory or non-contradictory. Marx construes contradictory recognition as property-based and non-contradictory (or mutual) recognition as pointing beyond property or what he calls existence in the mode of 'having' (Marx and Engels 1975a: 300). Third, these observations notwithstanding, there is – we admit – a sense in which Marx does on occasion picture property as an object. When he does so, however, the object concerned is – in conformity with the notion of contradictory recognition – one that is 'bewitched' and 'mystified'. The notion of property as a *bewitched object*, which underlies Marx's well-known passage on fetishism (Marx 1976: 163–6), can be developed in a number of directions: not least, the *situation in which such a bewitchment takes place* can be indicated. For Marx, the situation is above all one where a produced object has been expropriated (as in scenarios of exploitation) and the circumstances of this expropriation – recognitive relations – forgotten. This notion can be generalized: in Marx's view, conceptions of *objects* are to be approached through analysis of social relations. Human sensuousness, and thus conceptions of objectivity, exists 'through the *other* man' (Marx and Engels 1975a: 304).

To repeat, Marx thinks of property as a relation between individuals. But which individuals does he have in mind? Those whom he pictures are, first, the producer – private property 'results by analysis from the concept of *alienated labour*' (Marx and Engels 1975a: 279) – and, second, the owner. In both instances, property involves a diminution of human capacities. In the case of the producer, property involves being, so to say, on the receiving end of a relation of exploitation – and the 'one-sided and unequal' recognition that exploitation entails. For the producer, moreover, *being exploited* is an experience that intensifies over time: 'the more powerful labour becomes, the more powerless becomes the worker' (Marx and Engels 1975a: 273). To employ the terminology used in *Capital*, the rate of surplus value increases. The point is vital to our discussion because, as the power which stands *over against* the worker increases, contradictions to the worker's self-determination multiply.[8] If, now, we turn from the producer of property to its owner, we find that there too a diminution of human capacities is present. In the case of the owner, the many-sidedness of human sense-experience is reduced to a 'sense of *having*' (Marx and Engels 1975a: 300).[9] Stated differently, where ownership is involved, 'possessive individualism' (MacPherson 1962) rules. If both the producer and the owner of property are humanly diminished, the difference between them is in Marx's view massive: the 'propertied class' and the 'class of the proletariat' present 'the same human self-estrangement. But the former class feels at ease and strengthened in this self-estrangement . . . [whereas] the latter feels annihilated in estrangement; it sees in it its own powerlessness and the reality of an inhuman existence' (Marx and Engels 1975b: 36).

The passages which we have just quoted are to be found in Marx's work of the 1840s. In the first volume of *Capital* (published in 1867), the same cluster of themes is to be found. As already indicated, the worker's increasing powerlessness is foregrounded in the notion of a rising rate of surplus value. The implications of this rise are made explicit in the observation that, as capitalism develops, 'accumulation of wealth' at one pole of society is 'accumulation of misery [*Elend*]' at the other (Marx 1976: 799). In the *Grundrisse* and in *Capital*, owners are depicted as 'proprietors' – who, *as* proprietors, count as 'personifications [*Charaktermasken*] of economic categories' (Marx 1976: 92). The notion of *Charaktermasken* suggests both dissemblance and discomfort: a mask distorts and simplifies a living individual's face. And though the mask of dissemblance may sit more comfortably on the capitalist's face, a social world where any individual wears such a mask is a world of alienation.

Besides what it has to say on production and ownership, *Capital* explores the notion of *property as an object* in a distinctive way. It tells us that, in a world where there is commodity production, relations between individuals take on 'the fantastic form of a relation between things' (1976: 179, 1973: 243). Social relations, and individuals themselves, become thing-like (*dinglich*) – to the point where a market in labour power exists. Marx's 1844 comment on the worker 'as a *commodity*' and the central arguments of *Capital* say the same thing.

Our claim is that Marx's arguments, in 1844 and 1867 alike, are arguments concerning *recognition*. When Marx thinks of property not *in terms of the object* but *in terms of individuals' lives*, he is thinking of it in terms where recognition is in play. If it is asked how, in Marx's view, recognition enters the picture, our claim becomes more specific: for the producer and the owner of property alike, the recognition that property involves is (in the *Phenomenology*'s sense) contradictory. This is true of both the producer and the owner.

For the producer, the workplace – the 'hidden abode of production' – is a location where *one-sided and unequal recognition* prevails: this is so not merely because a boss patronizes or demeans workers but because, as *Capital*'s theory of surplus value makes explicit, one-sidedness and exploitation is intrinsic to commodity production. Surplus value and hence profit *just is* exploited labour. Likewise as a consumer, when the worker gazes upon capitalism's 'immense collection of commodities' (Marx 1976: 126) as a sum total of *what is unaffordable*, he or she confronts property as, in effect, a mass *of objects* that stands *over against* the individual. This occurs most palpably when even the essentials of subsistence lie beyond the individual's reach.[10] What he or she experiences is the *denial of self-determination* that contradictory recognition entails.

For the owner, property is (in present-day society) held in and through market relations – and the market is a social institution or system wherein (as in *any* institution) *role-definitional recognition* obtains. In the market, individuals recognize one another as 'proprietors' – as both the *Grundrisse* and *Capital* point out. The recognition which goes forward in the market is, being role-definitional, recognition of a contradicted or alienated sort. If the market is, for Marx, a social institution or 'spiritual mass' (Hegel), it *cannot but* be a site of recognition in a contradictory or alienated sense. Marx, we suggest, underlines the notions of contradiction and alienation through his metaphor of *Charactermasken*: if masks do not exactly 'fit' on to living faces, it is because *abstract universals* leave particular differences between individuals out of account.

If, now, the figures of the producer and the owner are considered together, the result is (we may note) a familiar image in Marx. To the 'hidden abode of production' – the workplace – there corresponds, for Marx, the juridical realm which presents itself as a 'very Eden of the innate rights of man' (1976: 280). The world of capital is, to borrow Hegel's words when describing post-Roman society, a 'world that is double, divided and self-opposed' (1977: 295). For Hegel in the *Phenomenology*, a 'double' world is a world divided into *geistige Massen*; our suggestion is that, for Marx, the realms of production and exchange are *geistige Massen* in the same sense. The world where the producer and the owner are, in Marx's expression, the dramatis personae is a world where alienation and contradictory recognition rule. It is a world of thinghood (*Dingheit*) – to employ an expression used both by Hegel (1977: 115) and Marx (1976: 165).

Let us stand back from our comments on Marx and property. How much has our argument achieved? Our claim is not that, for Marx, contradictory recognition *can only* appear through private property. It is that, in Marx's view, private property turns upon – and is therefore, to be understood in terms of – contradictory recognition. But have we supplied reasons for endorsing this claim? A critic of what has been said may argue as follows: 'You have shown that Marx's conception of property can, indeed, be interpreted in the way you favour. But *can* is not the same as *must*. Why should Marx's conception of property be understood in the *Phenomenology*-influenced way you suggest?' To such a critic, we reply that the reading we favour is, overwhelmingly, the most plausible. Marx's intellectual formation was that of a Left Hegelian, and his work – not least the *1844 Manuscripts* – shows an intimate knowledge of Hegel's *Phenomenology*. As demonstrated, even the terms which Marx employs – terms which are often missed by Marx's English translators – carry echoes of Hegel. Would it not be all-but-miraculous – a coincidence beyond reason – if Marx and the Hegel of the *Phenomenology* found themselves independently saying so closely related things?

The foregoing points can be developed further. Property gives rise to a specific – and erroneous – conception of *individuality*: surrounding the individual in a world of property, there is a *space* which may be narrow or roomy; at the outside edge of this space, a *boundary* obtains. Beyond this boundary, other individuals (who are similarly *bounded*) exist. Marx draws such a picture of bourgeois society in his early 'On the Jewish Question': in such a society, we learn, the 'limits [*Grenze*] within which anyone can move *without harming* someone else are defined by the law, just as the boundary [*Grenze*] between two fields is defined by a boundary post [*Zaunpfahl*]' (Marx and Engels 1975a: 364). This picture is immensely influential and long-lasting in bourgeois thought, from the time of natural law theory onwards. During the Enlightenment it reappears in Fichte's stipulation of 'a sphere for my freedom from which I exclude the other' (2000: 48), a notion explicitly criticized by Hegel (1977: 144–7). In the twentieth century it lives on in Isaiah Berlin's reference to an 'area within which a man can act unobstructed by others' and to a 'minimum area of personal freedom' (Berlin 2006: 34, 36). In the twenty-first century, Axel Honneth speaks of a 'sphere of freedom' (2018: Ch. IV). The idea has a practical parallel in the capitalist world: from the first enclosures of land to the gated communities of today's cities to the prosaic suburban house with its picket fence or garden hedge.[11]

This tenaciously influential conception of freedom is summed up in Marx's observation that 'the practical application of man's right to liberty is man's right to *private property*' (Marx and Engels 1975a: 163). It is because freedom – Marx is referring to the natural law tradition and its heir in liberalism – is taken to be human *property*, that it is conceived in spatial terms and as having bounded edges. An individual thus understood 'has' a 'sphere' of liberty within which, given certain provisos (typically the proviso not to encroach upon the spheres of others), they can do as they please. As a result, as Marx observes in the *1844 Manuscripts*, in ownership, a 'sense of *having*' engulfs all other human dimensions. The property owner, in short, becomes a *possessive individualist*.[12] If the tradition of aligning individuality and property (and thus cultivating a 'sphere of liberty') forms a cornerstone of liberalism, Marx is to be placed within an equally important counter-tradition – a tradition which, arguably, starts with Rousseau's *Discourse on the Origin of Inequality*[13] and continues through Hegel's critique of Fichte (see Hegel 1988: 144–7; Rauch 1983: 110–18) – that points up and castigates the *corrosive part played by the idea of property* in our conceptions of self and freedom.

Marx on class

We have argued that, for Marx, commodity exchange and property are instances of contradictory recognition. When a contrast between contradictory and mutual recognition is made the key, distinctive features of Marx's discussion spring to light.[14] Just as with commodity exchange, a bewitched or diabolically 'inverted' conception of mutual recognition is present in property relations. The *recognition presupposed by property* is, throughout, recognition of a contradictory (or, better, a contradicted) kind. Not until property relations are ended may uncontradicted recognition – mutual recognition in, so to say, a non-diabolical form – obtain. Our argument has a political implication: once approached in the light of *Phenomenology*-style recognition, it becomes clear that property *itself* – not just individual property but state-owned ('nationalised') property – is the target of Marxist critique.[15]

Here we present our own account of what Marx understands by class society. As a reader will be unsurprised to learn, we believe Marx understood class in recognition-based terms. Before demonstrating this, however, we note difficulties that arise from the traditional Marxist approaches to class – approaches from which we diverge.

(a) In traditional Marxist theory (as in non-Marxist sociology), it is widely supposed that social classes are groups of individuals. This supposition may, to be sure, be stretched in its application by allowing that (some) individuals have 'contradictory class locations' (Wright 1976). However, the term 'locations' suggests a problematic view of individuality: an individual is pictured as a being who occupies a specific amount of space – a specific amount of *bounded* space – which may or may not fit into a class understood as a container. The circumstance that individuals are pictured in this manner encourages us to think of 'contradictory class locations' as, so to say, *limiting cases* of the 'classes as groups of individuals' view. The view that *classes are groups of individuals* and the view that there may be 'contradictory class locations' share the assumption that – in Hegel's terminology – classes are abstract universals.

When *The Communist Manifesto* opens with the statement that the 'history of all hitherto existing society' is the 'history of class struggles' (1976b: 482), a reader is introduced to a dynamic and a pattern of activity which culminates in a form of society where mutual recognition prevails. If Marx was picturing *classes* as *groups of individuals*, his thought would turn on a notion of class-membership that involved *institutional (i.e. role-definitional) recognition*. The dynamic that pointed *beyond* contradiction, and towards mutual recognition, would remain enmeshed in an alienated (a contradicted or contradictory) world.

(b) For traditional Marxism, the following proposition has a quasi-axiomatic status: *class relations* are *relations of production*. An implication of the proposition is that an individual's class is decided by his or her place in the production process. Our response to this proposition is not straightforward and calls for comment at this stage.

Our initial response to the proposition is to say that class relations are, like all social relations, relations of recognition. Are the claims that *class relations are relations of production* and *class relations are relations of recognition* incompatible? We deny that this is the case. There need be no incompatibility because, we consider, relations of production – property relations, exchange relations and relations in the 'hidden abode of production' itself – can be analysed in a recognition-based way. Elsewhere in this chapter, we have dwelt on ways in which Marx offers such an analysis. Once it is seen that Marx, in his early and later writings, is focusing upon *contradictory recognition*, it becomes possible to speak of a 'monism of recognition' (see Chapter 3) which encompasses relations of production themselves.

This said, there is a sense in which the claims that *class relations are relations of production* and *class relations are relations of recognition* contradict one another. This sense is important, because it is present in a 'traditionally Marxist' view. The reading of Marx as a *theorist of 'base' and 'superstructure'* understands relations of production in a way where recognition can have no place. For this reading, relations of production are 'the economic structure of society, the real foundation, on which arises a legal and political [and ideological] superstructure' (1971: 20).[16] If relations of production are construed in the way this passage suggests, they count merely as 'economic'. By contrast, recognition, which turns on the notion of self-determining and totalizing individuals, cannot be pictured in merely 'economic' terms. Let us agree that, when seen in terms of the base-and-superstructure model, the claims that *class relations are relations of production* and *class relations are relations of recognition* are incompatible. We remove this incompatibility, and bring into focus Marx's overall discussion, by setting the metaphor of base and superstructure aside.

From alternative views, we turn to our own interpretation. How does Marx understand 'class'? Famously, the 'scientific [*wissenschaftlicher*]' (Marx 1976: 93) account of class that, it seems, *Capital* was to contain remains unfinished.[17] Where should a discussion of Marx on 'class' begin? Our approach is to start from very general features of what Marx terms 'hitherto existing society' – and then to work detail into the picture. As the picture becomes more specific, the notion of 'class' appears.

Might Marx's conception of 'hitherto existing society' be summarized in a diagram? On the face of it this seems doubtful: for Marx, the history of 'hitherto existing society' is the movement of contradiction – and contradictions, when presented diagrammatically, tend to disappear. If, however, this difficulty is disregarded, a schematic contrast can be drawn. Let us agree that the notion of *society* can, conventionally, be represented by a *closed circle*. Let us agree, further, that the figure's *closure* fits together with the idea of social integration. Can Marx's view of 'hitherto existing society' be pictured in this way? We deny that it can. While it is true that, for a society to exist, it must be capable of 'continual reproduction' (Marx 1976: 772), what is reproduced continues to be (until communism is achieved) contradictory existence. Stated differently, Marx's picture is one where social integration exists only in a fragile and problematic and 'at-issue' way. What characterizes 'hitherto existing society' is a dynamic – a dynamic of contradiction – which undermines 'continual reproduction' and springs social closure apart. If Marx's view of 'hitherto existing society' is to be given diagrammatic representation, an apt figure might therefore be *not a closed circle but an open parabola*. If the figure of an open parabola is to shed light on Marx's thinking, how might it be envisaged? We suggest that, if the parabola's opening is seen as *facing downwards* then striking features in Marx's view of 'hitherto existing society' appear.

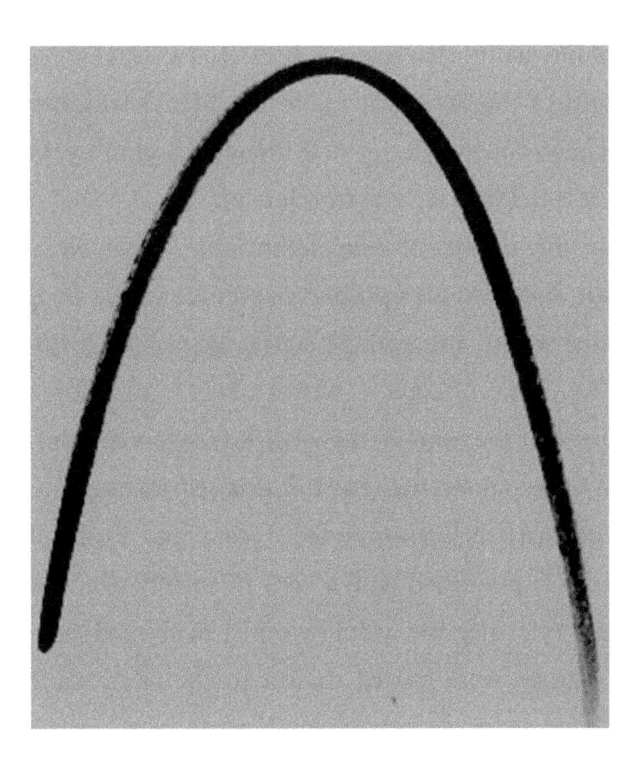

For Marx, life at the bottom of this 'inverted parabola' shades into a realm of 'thinghood' (*Dingheit*). Life as represented in the lower half of our diagram remains *through-and-through social* but is a realm of hell. It is a realm of 'misery' (Marx) where socially constituted human beings *count as things* and as nothing else. It is a region where there are 'material [*dinglich*] relations between persons' and 'social relations between things' (Marx 1976: 166). It is a realm where social relations are not *natural* but *quasi-natural* and exist in the mode of being contradicted or denied. The thought which our image of an open parabola attempts to capture is not that of social life in accordance with a natural order. It is that of social life where individuals are regarded *as though* they were merely natural and where, as a result, unimaginable horror – unimaginable *social* horror – is the result.[18]

What do our diagram-based reflections tell us about Marx? If the image of a downward-facing parabola is accepted, and interpreted as we have suggested, Marx comes forward as a theorist for whom vertiginous precipices of inequality characterize 'hitherto existing' social life. If our diagram captures (however schematically) Marx's conceptual picture, to look socially *downwards* is not merely to glimpse poverty and destitution, it is to look into a bottomless pit.

How may the notion of role definitions – that we emphasized earlier, in our discussions of property and exchange – be worked into the sketch that we are attempting? A passage written in 1845 supplies the clue. 'The property class' – writes Marx – 'and the class of the proletariat present the same human self-estrangement. But the former class feels at ease and strengthened in this self-estrangement. . . . The latter [by contrast] feels annihilated' (Marx and Engels 1975b: 36). There, a reader is presented with a view of society which we integrate into our 'parabolic' diagram as follows: just as, in medieval cathedrals, prestigious figures were buried closest to the altar, so, in a similar fashion, some role definitions (but not others) snuggle closely under our notional parabola's cusp. Bearers of such role definitions – role definitions which include 'capitalist' and 'proprietor' and 'burgher' – are, to use a familiar phrase, comfortable in their alienation. Further down the diagram, role definitions such as 'worker' are sites of oppression, discrimination and struggle. Beneath even the low-ranking role definitions are individuals who exist socially but who are, in terms of role definitions, nothing at all. In the bottomless pit, which the figure of an open parabola acknowledges, subsist the wretched of the earth – or the *proletariat*, in that term's etymological sense.

The social picture at which we arrive is arresting. At its top end, immediately under the cup of the parabola, exist individuals who have social standing. Such individuals are 'somebody' because their role definitions have a self-confirming status. To use a turn of phrase favoured by Marx, they are not merely *in* but *of* society. Further down the picture, role definitions entail less and less status – and more uncertainty about what the role definition means and how long it may be held. For how long, and with what degree of security, may one be a worker? Further still, what does it mean to be a refugee or a *sans-papier*? Of course *any* role definition implies *some* degree of standing – however minimal and uncertain this standing may be. It is when, following Marx, we continue downwards that the horror of existence that is *social* and yet *non-social* meets our gaze.

Having rounded out our discussion, we are in a position to draw conclusions. Marx, according to our all-too-schematic presentation, is in no way a theorist who operates in role-definitional terms. Role definitions (or *Charaktermasken*) receive discussion but as part of what is analysed: so to say, they are part of the problem rather than part of the solution. For Marx, role definitions float on a raft of recognition; the recognition is contradictory and dynamic. On the basis of our schematic discussion, we can say more about what this dynamic entails. Although role definitions present themselves as fixed and static and with clearly established boundaries, a deep and powerful current of *one-sided and unequal recognition* flows beneath them: issues of domination and struggle lie not *beyond their boundaries* but (changing the metaphor) *beneath the role-defined individual's feet*. Something of this sort is what Marx has in mind when he contrasts a realm of juridical appearance – a 'very Eden of the innate rights of man' – with the 'hidden' realm of production. It may even be what Marx has in mind when he introduces his ill-fated metaphor of 'base' and 'superstructure' – although, in this case, the 'base' is a pattern of recognition and the notion of a merely 'ideological' superstructure is exploded.

To equate 'class' with groups of individuals is, in effect, to see class *solely* in terms of role definitions – and thereby to become complicit in the alienation that institutional recognition entails. Our own view, which grounds 'class' in a dynamic of contradictory recognition, tells the whole social story – and presents role definitions as, so to say, reified ice floes that are carried on recognition's tide. To these remarks, a reader may raise an objection: Does our recognition-based view not leave *what is essential to 'class'* out of account? Surely a Marxist account of class must turn on ownership of the means of production? Let us agree that it does – but go on to say that the complex of themes discussed in this chapter highlights nothing else.[19] We do not downplay issues which the Marxist tradition has emphasized but, instead, approach these issues from a perhaps unfamiliar angle. For Marx, the notion of property (and thus ownership) contradicts the flow of recognition. Property *is* contradicted recognition. To move to a realm of social existence where recognition is uncontradicted is to stand the category of property on its head. It is true that we have not gone into detail about ways in which property has secured its dominion. We have not (so to say) traced the moves through which the game of domination is played. However, we have (we hope) shed light on the game's conditions.

Our conception of class has implications for how we understand *The Communist Manifesto*'s central terms: bourgeois and proletarians. How should the terms 'bourgeois' and 'proletarian' be understood? In the light of the present section, we can note an asymmetry between them: whereas the term 'bourgeois' echoes burgher or citizen and points to a role definition of some standing, the term 'proletarian' points to social existence *where there is nothing* – and slave-like *Dingheit* is the rule. In ancient Roman law, with which Marx was familiar, a 'proletarian' is someone who owns nothing (other than his children, who may be exploited) and who *is* nothing – in recognitive terms. A proletarian is too poor even to tax. Standing back from the Roman example and generalizing, if there is a 'proletariat', it does not qualify as an estate of the (republican or imperial or monarchic) realm. In terms of our diagram of an open and downward-facing parabola, if 'workers' are placed lower in our diagram than comfortable 'capitalists' and 'owners', proletarians are lower still – and subsist beneath the level where even the lowest or most lowly role definition is assigned. Proletarians are creatures of darkness.[20] When they *rise* – and the word is notable – they appear as hitherto non-existent beings. Those who capitalism leaves with 'nothing to lose but their chains' (Marx and Engels 1976b: 519) form not just a class but a multitude.

We have argued that, for Marx, *social relations are relations of recognition*. If social relations are, for Marx, relations of recognition, two points may be added. One is that both *one-sided and unequal recognition* and *institutional* (or 'role-definitional') *recognition* are fundamental to Marx's view of 'hitherto existing society'. Across the vertiginous precipices of an unequal society, contradictory recognition flows. The second point concerns the dynamic that is thereby present in Marx's (as in Hegel's) picture. If Marx's view of capital's dominion is a Hegelian one, then the same contradictions and the same fragility must accompany that dominion at every turn. Capital's rule cannot be other than crisis-ridden, fragile and breakable. While the master needs the slave, the slave does not need the master. The subjugated may at any moment revolt and claim their autonomy. The rattling of domination's chains is the sound of capital's death knell.

Marx on communism

The three previous sections of this chapter have explored contradicted recognition. They dwelt on what Marx terms 'hitherto existing society' (and what Hegel before him termed 'history'). Our final section looks beyond contradictory recognition and comments on how mutual recognition is seen by Marx. Our argument here is nothing less than that Hegel's mutual recognition and Marx's *communism* are one and the same thing.

Our starting point is the passage in Marx's *1844 Manuscripts* where communism is described as 'the real *appropriation* of the *human* essence by and for man' (Marx and Engels 1975a: 296). As is frequently the case in Marx's unpublished writings, a good deal of precise content is packed into a colourful piece of text. Let us start with 'man': elsewhere in the *Manuscripts*, Feuerbach is praised for making 'the social relationship of "man to man" the basic principle of theory' (Marx and Engels 1975a: 328). Human existence is, for Marx, intrinsically social – to the point that an individual's sensuousness 'exists as human sensuousness for himself through the *other* man' (Marx and Engels 1975a: 304). When Marx says that communism is, or involves, the appropriation of 'man', what he has in mind is, we propose, humanity's social existence. From 'man' we turn to 'the *human* essence'. By this phrase, Marx understands humanity's 'species being'. The term 'species being' (*Gattungswesen*) is, no doubt, capable of various interpretations, but, here, we take our clue from Marx's declaration that 'Man is a species-being . . . because he treats himself as a universal and therefore a free being' (Marx and Engels 1975a: 337).

A being counts as a species being when it is aware of itself – and of what, through its awareness, it may become. This *active becoming* is essential to species being, in Marx's estimation: a merely natural being (such as an animal) 'suffers' (Marx and Engels 1975a), or is passive, whereas a species being 'sees himself in a world that he has created' (Marx and Engels 1975a: 277). An animal 'is immediately one with its life activity' whereas man, as a species being, 'makes his life activity the object of his will and consciousness' (Marx and Engels 1975a: 276): in virtue of this non-coincidence with himself, 'man' may be a 'free being' (Marx and Engels 1975a: 275). We may sum up this line of thought by saying, that for Marx, humans are self-determining.

With these explanations in place, we may read or re-read the passage that is our starting point: if communism is 'the real *appropriation* of the *human* essence by and for man', it is the appropriation of man as a self-determining and social being. Let us agree that this is the case. It may be asked, however, how can human being be *both* self-determining *and* social? If an individual is seen as social, are there not limitations – so to say, communitarian limitations – on what he or she may think and do? If an individual is seen as self-determining, are social limitations not thrown to the winds?

If mutual recognition in the *Phenomenology*'s sense is brought into play, this last trace of the dichotomy between social and individual existence is surpassed. For the *Phenomenology*, as we have seen, individuals who mutually recognize one another 'enjoy perfect freedom and independence' (1977: 110). Conceptually, what allows the *Phenomenology* to see beyond a social-*versus*-individual dichotomy is the *constitutive* dimension of Hegelian recognition: because recognition is constitutive, individuals may be seen as free through the recognition that others give. In addition, the 'perfect freedom' which individuals enjoy is *freedom as self-determination* – rather than freedom understood in a merely 'freedom from' or 'negative' sense. This is so because, where mutual recognition obtains, *what* is recognized is the self-determining action that individuals perform.

It may be objected that the term 'communism' highlights sharing, whereas 'mutual recognition' points towards freedom. But the issues flow together: *free sharing* and *shared freedom* are different ways of saying the same thing. What is shared is a freedom that comes about through interaction, and freedom itself subsists in a dialogical or interactive way. When property (not just this or that species of property, but property per se) is dispensed with, individuality ceases to be monological and possessive, freedom ceases to exist *in spite of* other individuals (see Marx and Engels 1975a: 163), freedom exists in and through interaction with others and individuals risk their identity in mutual recognition's flow.

Such a view or vision has dark as well as light aspects. We start with the latter. Where mutual recognition obtains, each individual counts as free through the recognition that others provide – and from this stems an egalitarianism which schemes of social justice invoke. From this, too, stems a commitment to participatory democracy. (As we argue in Chapter 4, a participatory democracy which stems from mutual recognition has a 'consensual' – rather than a 'majoritarian' – cast.) A list of commitments entailed by mutual recognition can readily be extended. Not least, it can bring into focus ecological issues, as we argue in Chapter 5.

It is, for Marx, *because* communism and mutual recognition are the same that communism is valuable – in human and social and political terms. It is *because* communism is 'the real *appropriation*' of socialized humanity that communism is important. In Marx's view, mutual recognition is *in the last instance* communism's rationale.[21]

Are there further passages in Marx which adopt a recognitive position? We think there are. A number of them can be indicated here. First, Part One of Marx's 'On the Jewish Question' (1844) ends with an invocation of what is, in effect, mutual recognition. For Marx, an emancipated society is one where an individual is not an 'abstract citizen'; instead, the individual is a '*species being* in his everyday life'. In such a society, powers are directly 'social'. The individual 'no longer separates social power from himself' (Marx and Engels 1975a: 168). When Marx rejects abstract citizenship, and when he attacks powers that stand over against individuals, he turns to a pattern of social existence in which *species being* (or in other words self-determination) may thrive. How may *social* existence be *self-determining* existence? Each may exist through the other if mutual recognition obtains.

Next, we turn again to Marx's *Comments on James Mill* (1844), a text which envisages a situation where each individual affirms 'himself' and 'the other person' in his production (1992: 277). On the one hand, the individual thereby experiences his or her own 'personality' as 'objective' and 'visible to the senses': he or she sees himself or herself through the eyes of others and their personality is thereby 'confirmed'. On the other hand, the individual addresses 'the need of another'. The relation between the individual who addresses the other's need and the individual who is thereby addressed is, as Marx says, reciprocal or mutual. In this striking passage, Marx allows himself to use the term 'love' (1992: 277).

Moving forward in time, two well-known passages may be considered. In *The German Ideology* (1845), Marx looks towards a condition where the division of labour is abolished and I may 'do one thing today and another tomorrow, to hunt in the morning, fish in the afternoon, rear cattle in the evening, criticize after dinner, just as I have a mind, without ever being hunter, fisherman, shepherd or critic' (Marx and Engels 1976a: 47). The sting of this passage is in its tail: Marx does not, here, attack the notion of a *technical* division of labour (he allows that hunting and fishing and so forth are distinct activities) but is concerned with the role definitions – those of, for example, 'hunter' and 'fisherman' – that a *social* division of labour entails. The passage does, to be sure, picture a technical division where activities circulate swiftly – or more swiftly than is currently the case. The main thrust of Marx's words is, however, on role definitions as an issue. He anticipates a world where, in effect, role-definitional recognition is ended. Stated differently, he anticipates a world where mutual recognition is in play.

The second of the well-known passages refers to mutual recognition in all but name. In the closing sentence of *Communist Manifesto* Part II, Marx describes post-revolutionary society as 'an association, in which the free development of each is the condition for the free development of all' (Marx and Engels 1976b: 506). Such a description envisages a condition where each is free *through* (and not *in spite of*) their relations with others.[22] It pictures emancipation as mutual recognition.

In his subsequent writings, emancipation continues to be linked to an image of mutually recognitive existence. In *Capital*, Marx looks beyond commodities to 'an association of free men' (1976: 171) – one where 'the full and free development of every individual forms the ruling principle' (1976: 739). For the *Grundrisse* manuscripts of 1857–8, emancipation comes into being when 'communal production [*gemeinschaftliche Produktion*]' – indeed, 'communality [*Gemeinschaftlichkeit*]' – prevails (Marx 1973: 172). The themes of 'On the Jewish Question' and the

1844 Manuscripts are recapitulated. Such communal production involves 'the development of all [human] powers'; as such, it cannot be measured on 'a *predetermined* yardstick'. It reproduces human being not 'in one specificity' but in its 'totality' (Marx 1973: 488). Passages such as these carry forward, and restate, Marx's earlier views. Tacitly or explicitly, they draw upon mutual recognition as a theme. There is, in our view, no reason whatever to see Marx as turning against *Phenomenology*-inspired ideas.

Finally, we stand back from our discussion. Our overall argument is that Marx's thought turns on a contrast between contradicted and uncontradicted recognition. This contrast serves as, so to say, an armature around which Marx's more specific theorizing is arranged. Sometimes this armature is referred to explicitly. At other times, it is tacitly assumed. Whichever is the case, it is present – and gives his discussion a political edge. Proletarian revolution is, for Marx, a breaking away from one-sided and/or institutional recognition; it is a venture into a mutually recognitive realm.

We close with a question. What should be put in place of Marx's unfortunate 'base-and-superstructure' metaphor? Our answer is, instead of thinking of Marx as a theorist of base and superstructure, we should think of him as a theorist of recognition. In our view, recognition (by which we understand *Phenomenology*-style recognition) goes, socially, *all the way down*; there is nothing that is not in some way or other an issue of recognition. If our views are endorsed, recognition (which can be neither strictly 'economic' nor 'ideological') explodes the base-superstructure model. Here, we stress that reliance on the model becomes not merely conceptually impossible but *redundant*. Once *Phenomenology*-style recognition is placed at the centre of Marx's work, and allowed to pervade his discussion, a definitive break with base-and-superstructure thinking can be achieved. Sotto voce and semi-acknowledged dependency on the model of base and superstructure become a thing of the past.[23]

Is a remodelling of Marx and Marxism along the lines that we have sketched plausible? The history of ideas certainly suggests that it is. When Hegelians in the decades after Hegel's death divided into Right Hegelian (or Old Hegelian) and Left Hegelian (or Young Hegelian) schools,[24] the *Phenomenology*'s notion of mutual recognition became for the latter an image of emancipation. Edgar Bauer, for example, looked towards a 'free community' which would be 'beyond the state' (see Stepelevich 1983: 273–4). Max Stirner's *The Ego and His Own* championed a 'new freedom' which would encompass particularity and involve more than 'freedom from' (see Stepelevich 1983: 339, 343). Marx for his part talks of a 'true community' which is 'no abstract universal power standing over against the solitary individual' (1992: 265). Achieving it requires the 'overthrow of all relations in which man is a debased, enslaved, forsaken, despicable being' (Marx and Engels 1975a: 182).[25] Our suggestion that Marx models his notion of an emancipated society on Hegel's notion of mutual recognition fits directly with the spirit of the young Marx's times. Marx began his revolutionary life as a Young Hegelian and, despite his exile to London, remained faithful to his earlier ideas. He is famous for having broken with Young Hegelianism. He should, instead, be famous for having consistently upheld Young-Hegelian and Left-Hegelian emancipatory ideas.

3

Revolutionary or less-than-revolutionary recognition?

In the course of the last twenty years, the term 'recognition' has entered the lexicon of mainstream political theory. The present chapter takes issue with accounts of recognition which have become influential in these decades. Our criticism of such accounts is twofold: themes explored in Hegel's and Marx's pioneering accounts of recognition have been downplayed and, at the same time, the notion of recognition has been stripped of its revolutionary force.

Discussion in this chapter falls into three sections. In the first, we comment on Charles Taylor's attempt to link the notion of recognition to multiculturalism. In the second, we discuss Axel Honneth's attempt to use recognition to ground a post-Habermasian critical theory. Our aim in discussing these trends is not only to evaluate them on their own terms but also to make clear how far each diverges from the understanding of recognition in Hegel and in Marx. In the third section, we restate – contra both Taylor and Honneth – the idea of a *revolutionary* recognition.

The standpoint from which the present chapter is written may be briefly indicated. During the twenty years of political theory we are dealing with, Left Hegelianism (Marxism included) has undergone a period of eclipse. As part of this eclipse, recognition has come to be understood in less-than-revolutionary ways. Our book contributes to a Left-Hegelian resurgence. It does so by recollecting a perspective on recognition that neoliberal hegemony has all but concealed. The process whereby the term 'recognition' acquired academic respectability is, we suggest, one of domestification. In the same movement as it established itself in political theory, the term's revolutionary wings were clipped.

Before embarking on our comments to this effect, two prefatory notes are needed. The first is that the limitations of recent theorizing become fully apparent only when the history of 'recognition' as a concept – and, more especially, its place in Hegel's *Phenomenology of Spirit* and in Marx's work – is seen. Here a reader is pointed back to Chapters 1 and 2 of our book. The second concerns the claims which the present chapter makes. Our target is less-than-revolutionary accounts of recognition which prevail in recent discussion. This is not to say, however, that we regard recent treatments as altogether conformist. Nor is it to invoke a conception of revolution that is fixed in an *a priori* way. With regard to the first point, we do not intend to close the door on a politics of what Angela Davis terms 'radical' (as distinct from 'conventional' or 'superficial') multiculturalism (2012: 103–4). With regard to the second, we share Axel Honneth's view that critical theory turns on the notion of recognition – while disagreeing fundamentally with Honneth as to how recognition (and hence critical theory) is to be seen.

Recognition and multiculturalism

The first phase of recent discussion opens with the publication, in 1992, of Charles Taylor's highly influential essay 'The Politics of Recognition'.

There, Taylor argues that questions about 'distinct cultural identities' raise 'the issue of recognition' (Taylor 1994: 52, 63). And he assumes that, conversely, questions about recognition – at any rate, questions about recognition in the 'public' (as distinct from 'intimate') sphere (Taylor 1994: 37) – take the form of multiculturalist questions. A reader of Taylor's essay is left with the impression that issues of recognition and issues addressed by twentieth-century multiculturalism are one and the same. Can this equation of issues be defended?

A first ground for disquiet lies in turns of phrase which Taylor employs. In the course of his discussion, we learn that recognition is something that may be *given* (Taylor 1994: 36, 39) or *withheld* (Taylor 1994: 36, 38) or *demanded* (Taylor 1994: 42, 64), that it may be *lacked* (Taylor 1994: 26) and (when lacked) *searched for* (Taylor 1994: 70), and that it may (or may not) be *due* (Taylor 1994: 29, 36, 66). In the last of these instances – an instance where it is synonymous with *respect* (Taylor 1994: 42, 70) – recognition is understood as a moral desideratum. In the remainder, it is understood as a resource which may be present or absent. Taylor's characteristic turns of phrase portray recognition as a sort of entity (or quasi-entity) which *is what it is* and concerning which questions of fair distribution can be raised. In short, his phrases draw the notion of recognition onto the conceptual terrain of 'liberal' political theory; moreover, they predispose a reader to conflate recognition-based and multiculturalist issues. Are our critical comments justified? We think they are. Their justification becomes evident when it is noted that recognition was by no means always understood as something which *is what it is*, and which may or may not be present. As will be argued later, it was viewed as co-present with social existence and subsisting in contradicted or uncontradicted (or 'alienated' or 'non-alienated') ways.

To these comments, a note may be added. Taylor presents his claims as liberal in character – but as conflicting with liberalism of a specifically 'procedural' kind.[1] In the light of the phrases italicized in the preceding paragraph, it is tempting to qualify Taylor's disclaimer: his quarrel appears to be less with proceduralism's restriction to issues of fairness than with its failure to regard recognition as a resource which should be distributed in a fair way. Read thus, 'The Politics of Recognition' is more closely embedded in current forms of liberal theory than at first sight appears.

A second ground for disquiet is more overtly social and political. It concerns the notion of 'distinct cultural identities' – in effect, the unit of analysis which multiculturalism employs. We do not deny that, in the existing world, an individual's sense of identity may be mediated through his or her cultural grouping.[2] Nor do we deny that an individual's sense of identity is affected if his or her cultural grouping is viewed in a demeaning way. For us, however, the mediation of individual identity through distinct groupings (cultural or otherwise) is, itself, a seedbed of difficulties. Problems arise not merely when a group or culture is demeaned but when individual identity is seen as membership-based.

Why, it may be asked, should a membership-based view of individual identity be viewed with suspicion? Our aim is not, here, to rehabilitate an abstract or asocial view of the individual. It is, on the contrary, to uphold a view of individuality which is through-and-through recognitive and social.[3] Not the least of our reservations concerning a membership-based view of individual identity is that it clashes with conceptual and political potentialities that the notion of recognition contains.

Problems with membership-based views of individuality come into focus, we propose, when an individual's relation to his or her cultural group is considered. Two points especially strike us as significant. One is that a group or culture of which an individual is a member stands *over against* the individual concerned. While penetrating the individual's mind, and affirming its authority, the group is experienced as a predominant feature – sometimes a nurturing, sometimes a suffocating, feature – of his or her external world. The other point is that a sense of identity rooted in group-membership is, at best, incomplete. Only part of individuality is acknowledged. As, say, *a woman* or *a Muslim* or *a gay man*, an individual is recognized under a category which, although it has a specific or determinate content, applies alike to a range of disparate beings. So to say, such an individual is divided into *universal* (and acknowledged) and *particular* (and unacknowledged) aspects. Taken together, our points bring into focus an alienation which is not removed if the group concerned is valued in a positive or even-handed fashion. In order to grapple with *this* alienation, and move beyond it, what is needed (we claim) is a notion of recognition which thinks beyond a world where groupings of cultures into distinct identities are the order of the day.

Where do these comments leave Taylor's discussion? Passages in 'The Politics of Recognition' which reject the view that cultures *qua* cultures have 'equal worth' (Taylor 1994: 72, 64), and which advocate a 'fused horizon of standards' (Taylor 1994: 70), may be read as calling in question a membership-based conception of individual identity. This said, Taylor's article neither develops the notion of recognition beyond multiculturalism's concerns nor shows awareness of alienations which a membership-based identity may entail. If horizons are fused, in what sense (if any) do 'distinct cultural identities' continue? A reader of 'The Politics of Recognition' remains uncertain as to how its argument may proceed.

We turn to the literature on recognition and multiculturalism which emerged in the wake of Taylor's article. In part, we suggest, this literature raises familiar issues. One such issue concerns the terms in which recognition is to be seen. For Emcke and Fraser, for example, recognition is something that may be *claimed* (Fraser 1997: 129; Emcke 2000: 484; cf. Fraser and Honneth 2003: 46); for Tully, it makes sense to say that it may be *demanded* (Tully 2000: 473–4, 2004: 94) and *sought* (2000: 476). Such turns of phrase – all of which jar on the ears of a reader familiar with Hegelian and Marxist discussion – hint once again at a transposition of the notion of recognition onto liberal terrain.

Admittedly, the literature on recognition that has followed in Taylor's wake introduces fresh considerations. Two points in particular call for comment: (a) multiculturalism is understood in a broad fashion as a 'politics of identity and difference' (Markell 2003: 9; Thompson 2006: 186) and (b) attention is given to forms of grouping which may be of multiculturalist concern. For Emcke, for example, group-given identity may be 'chosen' or 'imposed' and must, in both cases, be seen in a 'historical context' (Emcke 2000: 485, 487). For Tully and Markell, identities rooted in group-membership are transformed by the struggles in which they are upheld (Tully 2000: 476–9; Markell 2000: 499). In effect, both writers insist that social and cultural groupings be viewed in a non-fixed-and-given and, so to say, non-essentialist way.

Do these considerations render our comments on alienation and group-membership inapplicable? We propose that (with a qualification that we shall mention) nothing is changed. Regarding point (a), the significance of a broadening of multiculturalism into a 'politics of identity and difference' depends on how the term 'difference' is viewed. If the term is taken to mean, merely, *difference between identities*,[4] the conceptual situation is unaltered. If, by contrast, difference is seen as *more fundamental* than identity, then an element of ambiguity is introduced. *Either* the identity, which is vested in groups, continues to be important (in the same way as actors on a stage may employ masks) *or* – and here comes our qualification – difference is seen as coming into its own only when notions of group-identity have been set aside. The latter may be Fraser's meaning when she refers to a 'shifting field of multiple differences' (Fraser and Honneth 2003: 76) as a social goal (Fraser and Honneth 2003: 74–5). Regarding point (b), the question of whether membership-identity involves alienation and the question of whether a group is (so to say) essentialist or non-essentialist are, we consider, conceptually distinct. Even a group which an individual has chosen to join, and even a group which has no fixed or given essence, is one which stands *over against* the individual. A group which an individual has chosen, and is open to change over time, remains one where membership divides an individual into *what is particular* and *what is universal*. No doubt, the fixed-and-given status of a group may intensify the alienation that membership in it involves. But the source of the alienation lies in the existence of identity-prescribing social groupings per se.

Besides commenting on the circumstance that groups change their nature through multiculturalist struggle, Tully and Markell argue for positions which demonstrate their distance from what in our view counts as a recognition-based approach. Tully urges that 'agonic democratic games over recognition and distribution' admit of no definitive resolution; what matters, in his view, is that the 'games' (a term he employs in a Wittgensteinian fashion) are freely played (2000: 469, 474, 477; see also Tully 2004: 91, 98). At one point in expounding the nature of these 'agonic games', Tully describes it as 'unfortunate' that 'the Hegelian term "recognition" has been used to characterize and study them': Hegel's term suggests that there is an 'end-state' where all concerned obtain the 'form of mutual recognition' which they 'demand' – and this is a 'dangerous illusion' (Tully 1999: 175). Our response to this passage is twofold. The first concerns Tully's judgement that multiculturalism's appropriation of the term 'recognition' is 'unfortunate': while agreeing that it *is* unfortunate, we note that Tully's reason and our own for considering that this is the case are diametrically opposed. Our own view is that, in such an appropriation, the wings of the term are clipped: recognition, as seen through a multiculturalist lens, makes its peace with an alienated world. Tully's contrasting view is that agonic struggles promote 'identification' with the 'democratic society which enables them to take place freely' (Tully 2000: 480) – and that this 'identification' is a good thing. In other words, he sees agonic struggle in a socially integrative light. Our second response to the passage cited concerns mutual recognition. Mutual recognition in its Hegelian meaning is not, we propose, a resource which may be distributed – whether in a satisfactory or an unsatisfactory fashion. It is a mode of existence linked to the freedom that open interaction brings.

For Markell, the view that multiculturalist struggles change 'group identities' (2000: 499) is linked to a stress on the 'finitude' of human existence: aspirations to 'independence and sovereignty' are futile, Markell contends, and a recognition-based perspective must be understood as a reminder that all humans are *dependent on others* (2000: 505, n. 12; 2003: 10–11). In Markell's view, moreover, the notion of recognition is bound up with an 'ontological misrecognition of the nature and circumstances of our own activity' (2000: 503). Our response to such comments is to emphasize that we neither affirm a socially unreal individual 'independence' nor concede, with Markell, that *dependence* (of one sort or another) is all that may be politically achieved. Instead, we point to a freedom (or 'independence') that exists – or may exist – *in and through* relations with others. Such a view of freedom is, we argue, made possible if the notion of recognition is understood in a revolutionary way.

Recognition in Honneth

In the second phase of recognition's incorporation into political theory, the focus of discussion shifts: whereas Taylor's essay links recognition to multiculturalist issues, Axel Honneth's *The Struggle for Recognition* (German edition 1992; English translation 1995) explicitly relates the notion to critical theory. The expression 'critical theory' has, of course, different meanings. In Max Horkheimer's classic formulation, it meant theorizing whose 'goal is emancipation from slavery' (1972: 246). It meant, in other words, theorizing with a revolutionary aim. When Honneth, director of the same Frankfurt Institute for Social Research once headed by Horkheimer, turns to the notion of recognition in critical theory's name, a reader may expect that he aims to further just such a theorizing. Does Honneth's understanding of recognition live up to this expectation? In what follows it will become clear that this is not the case.

A critical discussion of recognition as a theme in Honneth may have a number of starting points. One is (as in Taylor) the phraseology that it employs. Honneth speaks of recognition as something that may or may not be *justified* (Honneth 2007: 325), and which can be *withheld* (Honneth 2007: 325) or *claimed* (Fraser and Honneth 2003: 133, 134). He frequently uses the term 'recognition' (*Anerkennung*) interchangeably with 'esteem' or 'appreciation' (*Wertschätzung*) (e.g. Honneth 2018: 32, 148). In short, his theorizing is coloured by assumptions made in recognition's multiculturalist phase. Another starting point is Honneth's relation to the original critical theory tradition of Horkheimer (and Adorno and Marcuse): Is that tradition's 'critical edge' not 'blunted' – as Deranty proposes, and as we ourselves agree – in Honneth's writings? (Deranty 2004: 298, 316). A third possibility is to move directly to Honneth's distinction between three *patterns* or *forms* or *spheres* or *fields* of recognition, terms he uses interchangeably (1995: 92, 2013: 3, 4; Fraser and Honneth 2003: 137, 138, 142, 146, 155, 184, 187). Although (we suggest) any one of the just-mentioned approaches leads to a similar conclusion, we adopt the last mentioned in what follows.

In a wide range of his writings, Honneth draws a 'tripolar' (Fraser and Honneth 2003: 185) distinction between (a) recognition as 'love', (b) recognition as legal 'respect' and (c) recognition as 'solidarity' or 'esteem' or 'achievement' (see, for example, 1995: 92, 2007: 337, 2005: 46; Fraser and Honneth 2003: 138ff., 180; cf. Thompson 2006). Questions can be raised about each of the terms thus distinguished. Regarding (a), can 'love' be regarded as an instance of recognition, as Honneth suggests? On the one hand, recognition is frequently seen as requiring reciprocation – and Honneth appears to agree that this is the case.[5] On the other hand, object-relation psychoanalysis, to which Honneth appeals, views a mother's love as turning on 'identification of herself with her infant' (Winnicott 1990: 54) – and this identification is strictly one way. How should this clash of views be resolved? One way is to concede that love is not an instance of recognition – but, say, a *feeling*. Another is to see love as an instance not of recognition *sans phrase* but of recognition in a contradictory form. Regarding (b), should legal respect – more fully stated, equal respect for rights that may be enshrined in law – be viewed as an instance of recognition? Evidently, an answer to this question depends on how recognition is seen. Here, we offer only some passing observations. Does not law (whatever its content) stand *over against* an individual who is obliged to follow it? Is not law a 'blunt instrument' whose whole point is to address individuals as *universals* – as *citizens*, say, or indeed as *human beings* – and to set all that may be *particular* about them aside? The circumstance that such questions can be raised suggests that – as in the case of cultural groupings, discussed earlier – the standpoint of legal respect is one of contradictory recognition:

it belongs in an alienated world. Regarding (c), here, we propose, difficulties are still more entrenched – and are revealed by Honneth's shifting terminology. Why should 'solidarity' and 'esteem' be equivalent ideas? Honneth's answer to this question is to introduce the term 'achievement' – and to suggest that 'achievement' be understood as 'the extent of one's individual contribution to social reproduction' (Fraser and Honneth 2003: 263). The larger an individual's social contribution, Honneth seems to say, the more socially *esteemed* the individual may be. Our response to this argument is twofold. First, we deny that recognition (in its Hegelian sense) is synonymous with esteem. As we argued in Chapter 1, the notion of esteem presupposes particular personal qualities or actions which are deemed estimable. This (circular) form of argumentation is conspicuously absent in Hegel's *Phenomenology* which, by contrast, understands recognition to be recognition of *self-determination*. Second, we note that even if recognition is taken to be interchangeable with 'solidarity', 'esteem' and 'achievement', a distinctive feature of capitalist society is that it throws the very notion of esteem based on 'contribution to social reproduction' to the winds.

Although these points strike us as serious, the most controversial features of Honneth's discussion are general in character. Quite apart from what is said under the headings of 'love' and 'respect' and 'esteem', it may be asked, can recognition be seen (without distortion) as grouped into *spheres*? Our reply to this question is that it cannot. In existing society, let us agree, a grouping which (in outline at least) resembles Honneth's is present. But the notion of recognition is far from exhausted by such a grouping. When understood in the sense developed in this book, the notion of recognition challenges, and points beyond, a world where social spheres obtain.[6]

The difficulties that we see in the idea of 'spheres' of recognition run parallel to difficulties, raised earlier, concerning cultural groupings.

We have suggested that a cultural grouping stands *over against* an individual who is its member; in the same way, we propose, a sphere of recognition – familial love, legal respect, social esteem – stands *over against* an individual caught up in recognition which takes the form concerned. We have further suggested that membership in a cultural group divides an individual into *universal* and *particular* aspects. Here, we propose that 'spheres' as envisaged by Honneth acknowledge individuals only as *something* – as, say, a *family member* or *legal person* or *citizen* – and thus merely as the bearer of this or that universal social role. In short, spheres of recognition involve alienations similar to those that cultural groupings entail. In discussing cultural groupings, we suggested that the dynamic of mutual recognition must go beyond the alienations concerned. Here, in parallel fashion, we propose that the route beyond sphere-specificity is one which our revolutionary notion of recognition charts.

If these comments on sphere-specificity carry conviction, should we conclude that Honneth sanctions alienations which present-day society contains? For two reasons, such a conclusion may strike a reader as unfair.

First, Honneth draws a distinction between 'spheres of recognition' and 'institutional complexes' (Fraser and Honneth 2003: 146). He criticizes Hegel's *Philosophy of Right* – a work which he otherwise admires – for its 'institutionalist way of thinking' and 'harmonious closure' (Fraser and Honneth 2003: 145–6). If 'spheres of recognition' are not synonymous with 'institutional complexes', are we misguided in accusing Honneth of sanctioning alienation? To this question, we respond that the difference should not be exaggerated. How might a 'sphere of recognition' be pictured, other than as a complex of social relations which stands *over against* the individual? If an individual is caught up in a 'sphere of recognition' in the sense that it defines his or her identity, does he or she not confront, simply as a datum of experience, the circumstance that the sphere is one of love or esteem or respect? In short, does the notion of 'spheres of recognition' not already *prepare the way* for the reification of recognition into social institutions? This line of thought may, we consider, be carried a step further. If spheres of recognition exist, are individuals not acknowledged as *something* (or as *some things*) in ways where universality and particularity are severed? We have seen earlier, in our comments on law as a 'blunt instrument', that Honneth's discussion of legal respect generates difficulties about the relation between an individual's universal and particular aspects. Here, we suggest that *whether or not the sphere concerned is a legal one*, a sphere-specific view of recognition generates a dislocation between universality and particularity. The distinction which may be quoted in Honneth's favour fails to notice problems with which spheres *qua* spheres are beset. Despite his criticisms of Hegel's *Philosophy of Right*, Honneth still moves within that work's orbit.

Second, Honneth concedes that his book *Struggle for Recognition* tends to be phrased as though 'there are three stable forms of recognition which are universal'; but, he says, his later work tries to 'historicize the forms and spheres of recognition' (2013: 2).[7] The point is an important one in the present connection: if the spheres of recognition emphasized by Honneth are specific to capitalism, they may be seen as part of society's problem (rather than the form which a solution must take). So to say, a conceptual space opens where Honneth's discussion may regain what Deranty terms a 'critical edge'.

However, we doubt whether Honneth's historicization renews this critical edge. As a means of explaining these doubts, let us picture two contrasting, and highly schematic, accounts of history. According to one, history's crucial and, so to say, most traumatic transition lies in a passage from alienated to non-alienated existence. For Hegel, who shared this conception, the passage was one from history to post-history – and was signalled by the French Revolution (Hegel 1977: 6–7, 355–63; Hegel 1956: 447). For Marx, the passage was one from 'prehistory' to history proper, and comes about with the attainment of communism (Marx 1971: 20). According to the other, history's most crucial transition is that from pre-modern society to modernity. If problems concerning modernity exist, and if the notion of a transition from modernity to emancipated existence remains meaningful, such problems are – so the latter account affirms – relatively minor and residual in nature. Prospective changes to the status quo are seen as reformist (rather than revolutionary) and ameliorist (rather than fundamental). This view of history is indebted not to Hegel and Marx but to Weber. Its chief exponent in recent decades is Habermas.[8] Our doubt concerning Honneth's invocation of history is that, whereas the historical periodization employed by the early Frankfurt School critical theorists was that of Hegel and Marx, the periodization associated with Honneth's claims is Weberian.

In an interview by Goncalo Marcelo, Honneth refers to his 'debate with Nancy Fraser' – that is, *Redistribution or Recognition?* – as a work where the role of history is made especially clear (Honneth 2013: 3). What is striking in the present connection is that the most sharply focused historical passage in *Redistribution or Recognition?* concerns the 'differentiation of three spheres of recognition' – a differentiation which marked the transition from the pre-modern (or 'traditional') to the modern (or 'post-traditional') world (Fraser and Honneth 2003: 138, 140). The theme of post-traditional 'differentiation' – in contrast to a previously undifferentiated (although estate-specific) notion of 'honour' – is a recurrent one in Honneth's discussion.[9] Whereas the story told in this and similar passages is conceptually clear, the treatment of ways in which a three-sphere recognitive framework might change (and a transition from the status quo to an emancipated society might appear on the agenda) is impenetrable to a degree. From the interview just cited, we gather that changes in a sphere of recognition may result from a dynamic that is 'internal' or from influence exercised by 'other institutions of recognition' (Honneth 2013: 3–4). Is this internal/external distinction coherent? In a world where there is more than one sphere or recognition, internal change may open a sphere to external influence and external influence may accompany internal change. In such a world, can a line between *what is internal* and *what is external* be drawn? And where may the source of change (be it internal or external) lie?

From the corresponding pages of *Redistribution or Recognition?* (Fraser and Honneth 2003: 184–9) we gather that attaining a 'higher degree of individuality' is a fundamental motive in bringing about change in recognitive relations: this was the case when differentiation into three spheres of recognition took place at the start of the modern period,[10] as well as when (in the present) 'new borders between the individual spheres of recognition' are drawn (Fraser and Honneth 2003: 188; see also 189). But how is this fundamental motive to be understood? At times, Honneth appears to picture attaining a 'higher degree of individuality' as a direct concern of individuals introducing change – say, by redrawing the boundaries of spheres. When such concern is present, the change inspired may – let us agree for the sake of argument – be change of a revolutionary sort. At other times, however, the emphasis of Honneth's discussion turns on the notion of what he terms 'surplus validity' and it is unclear how, in his view, the themes of surplus validity and an increase in individuality are to be combined (Fraser and Honneth 2003: 174, 186).

Let us explain. For Honneth, a sphere of recognition has 'surplus validity' when it allows individuals 'to make other claims with reference to the same principle' (2013: 3). For example, the sphere of legal respect may be extended to justify welfare provision. A difficulty with basing demands on the notion of surplus validity is that, as Renault expresses the point, 'political struggles have to restrict themselves to the achievement of what the actual social order promises us. . . . Social progress can no longer be understood in qualitative terms, in terms of social transformation, but only in quantitative terms, in terms of amelioration' (Renault 2011: 216). In short, a politics based on the notion of surplus validity merely promises more of the same. When Honneth refers to the notion of 'surplus validity', his concern is – we may note – to ensure that critique is immanent. While his concern is, surely, respect-worthy, the way in which he fulfils it elides *immanence* with *continuity*: he fails to notice that terms suggesting a break with a principle (rather than a more consistent application of it) may best articulate a response to what socially and politically exists.[11] In the light of these comments, we may say that, whereas an appeal to the notion of a 'higher degree of individuality' may be revolutionary, a politics that bases itself on the notion of surplus validity is reformist at best. The question of how Honneth proposes to combine the notions is one of political as well as of conceptual interest.

Our claim is that, on this politically vital question, Honneth remains ambiguous. If anything, he tends to weigh his discussion on the 'surplus validity' side. A case for redrawing the boundaries of recognitive spheres must first, it seems, be made out in terms of surplus validity; 'only then . . . in a second step' may questions of individuality be brought into play (Fraser and Honneth 2003: 186). The notion of individuality may help us to 'pick out morally justified particularities from the multitude of those typically asserted in social struggles' but – and here Honneth's exposition is at its murkiest – the 'particularities' themselves seem to be ones which the notion of surplus validity has generated (Fraser and

Honneth 2003: 187). As it were, Honneth thinks of surplus validity and increased individuality as lexically ordered considerations. Stated differently, issues may be addressed in a revolutionary fashion only when consistent application of existing moral principles has made them count as topics of political concern. Our worry is that such a lexically ordered understanding of the case for revolution makes the notion of far-reaching social change problematic. This worry is intensified once we note Honneth's addition to the passage under consideration: there will, he tells us, 'always be a need to maintain the separate spheres' – and this separation is to be maintained, 'all the moral legitimation for boundary-shifting notwithstanding' (Fraser and Honneth 2003: 189). The transition from pre-modernity to modernity establishes (it seems) the limits of what is possible in the present-day political world.

On Honnethian premises, in other words, the status quo is unchanging in its fundamentals – and this circumstance has an implication for how critical theory is seen. For Honneth, the critical theorist must take the horizons of the present as fixed and given and recommend only non-structural improvements or alterations. Our own understanding of critical theory is quite different. A Hegelian rather than a Honnethian understanding of recognition bursts open the boundaries of what is possible politically. It blazes a trail to revolutionary transformation and in so doing redeems the original aim of critical theory.

So far we have concentrated on Honneth's conceptions of recognition and of history – and found these to be 'less than revolutionary'. There is, however, a further dimension to Honneth's work that makes its less-than-revolutionary character clearer still. In his *Freedom's Right*, the work in which Honneth presents his latest and most systematic discussion of recognition, he follows what he terms the 'methodological procedure of normative reconstruction' (Honneth 2014: 7). What does he mean by this?

On the face of it, 'normative reconstruction' seems a laudable attempt to restate the notion of immanent critique in its Frankfurt School and Marxian[12] sense. Immanent critique proceeds without *a priori* ethical standards, instead unfolding its values from the criticized object (here, existing society) itself. However, a closer look indicates that 'normative reconstruction' is markedly different. 'To normatively reconstruct', Honneth tells us, means analysing 'whether and how culturally accepted values are . . . realized in various different spheres of action, and which norms of behaviour ideally prevail' (Honneth 2014: 64). It is to look not to the contradictions in institutions but to their ideal form: the 'promise of freedom' they contain (Honneth 2014: 330).

Such a procedure, we feel, gets the situation back to front. It asks that the social critic or revolutionary activist start from (so to say) the best side of what existing society offers or claims to offer. It succumbs to a danger latent in immanent critique: staying so close to the criticized object that it fails to break with or overcome it. In a word, such a procedure risks losing critique's critical character altogether. And this, we suggest, is what occurs with Honneth's 'normative reconstruction': immanent critique becomes *so* immanent that critique all but disappears. An example can serve as illustration. When applied to capitalism, normative reconstruction requires, Honneth says, that we proceed 'in an idealizing manner', to uncover 'the path in the historical development of the capitalist market' that has led to a 'gradual realization' of 'social freedom' (2014: 197). This means, he continues, that the exploitation of wage labour should not be viewed as a '[s]tructural deficit which can only be removed by abolishing the capitalist market economy' but rather as a 'deviation' from the 'the market's own normative promise' (Honneth 2014: 196). In other words, Honneth sees no logical reason why the capitalist market could not become a realm free of exploitation and unfreedom. Such an approach, it goes without saying, is a far cry from Marx.[13]

Is there an alternative way to undertake critique? We suggest there is. It is to focus, as Brecht put it, not on the 'good old things' but on the 'bad new ones' (cited in Benjamin 1998: 121). It is to dwell on what, in existing society, is insufferable, atrocious or diabolical. It is to begin with what Marcuse calls a 'refusal' (Marcuse 1968: 200) or a 'scream', to employ John Holloway's vivid expression (Holloway 2005: 1). Such expressions point to a politics not of reform but of resistance, rebellion and revolt (see Hardt and Negri 2012: 31). They point, that is, to a social rupture which is anathema to a method that concentrates on society's best and brightest and seemingly most humane side.[14] Though revolution is destined to draw its values from what is latent in existing society, this need not involve looking fixedly on society's most positive or promising side. It can involve noting harsh juxtapositions and letting contradictions move.

We end our discussion of Honneth by noting a point where we (with qualifications) agree with his claims. In his disagreement with Fraser over the question of whether social issues require a '"two-dimensional" conception of justice' (as Fraser proposes) or whether a '"normative monism" of recognition' is needed (Fraser and Honneth 2003: 3), we ourselves are on Honneth's side of the debate. This is so because such a stance chimes with the Hegelian position we expound in this book: there is nothing social that is not in some way an issue of recognition. Not the least of the places where we sympathize with Honneth in the Fraser/Honneth exchange is in Honneth's charge that Fraser's notion of 'participatory parity' has roots in liberal political theory. If the notion of 'participatory parity' makes sense, Honneth counters, this is because a notion of mutual recognition is already presumed (Fraser and Honneth 2003: 176, 261–2). However, in pointing to topics where we feel agreement or sympathy, we are not indicating any deep endorsement of Honneth's position. On the contrary, if a recognition-based 'monism' is to be affirmed in connection with social issues, the recognition concerned cannot be understood in Honneth's – or, indeed, in multiculturalism's – sense. If critical theory is to be defended by basing itself on the concept of recognition, 'recognition' as a category must venture beyond Honneth's 'modernity'-inspired understanding of the term.

A return to revolutionary recognition

When set alongside the revolutionary idea of recognition we saw in Hegel and Marx (Chapters 1 and 2) a reader can now see how domesticated and hidebound this notion has become in Taylor's and Honneth's hands. Taylor's notion of recognition as a way to supplement a politics of rights with a politics of cultural difference along with Honneth's notions of 'recognitive spheres', of 'normative reconstruction' and of a history that all but ends in the transition to modernity are, taken together, ideas that clip recognition's revolutionary wings. Our aim in discussing the 'recognitive turn' in recent political and social theory is not only to show its weaknesses but also to show an alternative: to recover recognition's original meaning. Our aim is to reopen a path to a revolutionary notion of recognition that currently lies hidden behind a tangled undergrowth of liberal and recent Frankfurt School debate. Such an obfuscation of the meaning of recognition might perhaps be expected from liberal political thought; when undertaken in the home of critical theory, it is particularly regrettable.

To survey the terrain of so-called Frankfurt School theory today is to observe a very different landscape to that of the heyday of the Institute for Social Research and of critical theory. That heyday saw an explosion of radical and challenging ideas and – despite the occasional pessimism of a Horkheimer or an Adorno – a lasting commitment to revolutionary thinking. Such descriptions fit uncomfortably with recent Frankfurt School theorizing. In recent decades a decisive shift has taken place from the philosophies and politics of the Frankfurt School's founders. Honneth's work presents itself as renewing critical thought, yet, we fear, provides little more than an intricate philosophical justification for reform over revolution. It seems no coincidence to us that Honneth's most directly political book, *The Idea of Socialism* (2015), fires a broadside at Marxism and champions the same core values as the German Social Democratic Party.[15] To us, it becomes ever clearer that recent Frankfurt School thought has traded in a Marxist philosophy for a social democratic, that is, a reformist, ameliorist and institution-oriented world view.[16]

We began with Taylor's liberal foray into multicultural issues, a view that equated recognition with respect for cultural identities. We showed how such a view is unable to pose questions of the alienation involved in cultural identity. Honneth at first glance seemed to go beyond Taylor's limitations, but his appropriation of recognition for Frankfurt School thought succumbed to similar problems. In the different strands of the less-than-revolutionary discourse on recognition we see a common failure to think beyond the contradictory forms of recognition which pervade the present world – forms which Hegel's *Phenomenology* and Marx's writings exposed and criticized. It is no coincidence that the alienating aspect of human identities based on culture- or group-membership goes relatively unnoticed in Taylor's work while the alienated character of institutions and social spheres goes largely uncriticized in Honneth's: this is, we suggest, the high price paid for severing recognition from its original Hegelian meaning.

Standing back, we note that in these various recent appropriations of recognition the boundaries between critical theory and liberalism have become increasingly blurred. In Frankfurt, for instance, the vocabulary of liberal political philosophy seems to have won out over the rich Hegelian–Marxist thought-world in which the early Frankfurt School moved. This has political implications. Where the Frankfurt School in its heyday could place revolutionary ideas in the hands of a generation of political activists, it is hard to see the work of their successors having a similar effect. One outcome of our discussion may be to indicate – via a recovery of the original revolutionary meaning of recognition – how a revival of critical theory might proceed. When freed from current dogma, recognition can help ground a critical theory in its original radical sense.

At the beginning of the twenty-first century, in an era of global uprisings and renewed struggles, theory has little excuse for being out of step with the radical spirit of the times. If one is to look for a resonance of the idea of recognition in the contemporary world one might well observe the recent global uprisings, the 'Occupy' movement and the various prefigurative and mutualist social experiments that have followed it. Common to the various social movements that have risen to prominence in recent years is that they not only refuse an unjust, unfree and unsustainable social world but also attempt – through their forms of participation and ways of thinking – to bring into existence an entirely new one. It is no coincidence that these movements eschew institutions and particular cultural allegiances. These uprisings exemplify, in our opinion, what is central to Hegel's *Phenomenology* and Marx's work: contradicted and alienated recognition striving to become mutual recognition. However tentative and interstitial, the new politics visible in these movements are living examples of mutually recognitive interaction, islands of mutual recognition in an alienated social world.

4

Mutual recognition in practice

A reader who has followed us thus far may form an erroneous impression of our claims. He or she may decide that Gunn and Wilding offer a convincing or unconvincing argument that concerns the history of ideas. In part, we do indeed put forward a history-of-ideas argument. Our chapters on Hegel and Marx draw attention to lines of thought that orthodox Hegelianism and orthodox Marxism miss. We claim that, once the theme of recognition is highlighted, the relation between Hegel and Marx appears in a distinctive light. In the preceding chapter, we explored recent (liberal and Honnethian) discussions of recognition and concluded that the phrase 'less-than-revolutionary' captures their political spirit. In the light of our earlier discussion of Hegel and Marx a reader can now see why a return to the original meaning of recognition is needed and that the current usage of the term is to be abandoned.

But the question remains to be answered: Can the revolutionary view of recognition championed by Hegel and Marx do service not merely within the history of ideas but in the practical world? Can what we have called Hegel's 'dangerous idea' do political work here and now, at a time when *geistigen Massen* adopt a neoliberal guise? Can the notion of mutual recognition conceived by Hegel and developed by Marx help us picture and work towards a liberated society? If so, what would that society be like?

Hegel and Marx are famous as critics of utopianism. Hegel, in the preface to his *The Philosophy of Right* of 1821, opines that his book, as a work of philosophy, must be as far removed as possible 'from any attempt to construct a *state as it ought to be*' – his reason being that 'philosophy . . . is *its own time apprehended in thoughts*' (Hegel 2008: 15, emphasis in original). In 1880, Engels wrote *Socialism: Utopian and Scientific*, a work which sought to present Marxism as 'scientific' in the sense that the positivistic nineteenth century held dear. To be scientific, Engels believed, was to analyse what *is*, not what *ought to be*. Yet despite the political caution of Hegel's *Philosophy of Right* and the anti-utopian stream in Marxism, glimpses of what an emancipated existence might involve can be found in the work of both Hegel and Marx. This becomes clearer still in Left – or 'Young' – Hegelianism. Edgar Bauer, for example, favoured a 'free community' where critique came into its own (Stepelevich 1983: 70–4). Moses Hess believed that 'absolute freedom' and 'social equality', 'German atheism' and 'French communism' needed to be 'united' (Hess 2004: 105). For Max Stirner, a 'free association' and an 'Association of Egoists' were the same thing (see McLellan 1980: 128). Marx, for his part, cuts through the differences between Left Hegelians when he characterizes communist society as 'an association, in which the free development of each is the condition for the free development of all' (1976b: 506). In doing so, he laid bare the mutually recognitive basis of Young-Hegelian emancipation for all to see.

One of Marx's views of an emancipated future concerns us here. In *The German Ideology*, written jointly by Marx and Engels, there is a passage that demands attention. There, Marx and Engels refuse to consider communism as 'a state of affairs' (1976a: 49), but instead call it 'the real movement which abolishes the present state of things' (1976a: 49). If we feel the force of these remarks, important implications follow for how mutual recognition in practice is to be seen.

Hierarchy or horizontalism?

One implication is worthy of discussion here. If mutual recognition in practice is linked to the 'movement which abolishes the present state of things', it is inevitable that our chapter will overlap with the 'problem of organization' debated by Lenin and Luxemburg in the twentieth century's early years. We admit that, if we are compelled to choose between these two theorists, our sympathies lie with Luxemburg. Lenin (in his 1902 work *What Is to Be Done?*) assumes that political consciousness 'can be brought to the workers *only from without*', only from 'outside . . . the sphere of relations between workers and employers'. It can, in other words, only be inculcated by a vanguard party (1969: 98). The centralism, hierarchy and discipline of the vanguard party, along with the division of labour between 'cadre' and 'rank and file', are for Lenin the undemocratic price to be paid in the here and now for the future goal of a socialist democracy. Luxemburg strongly objected to Lenin's view, arguing that 'socialist democracy is not something which begins only in the promised land after the foundations of socialist economy are created; it does not come as some sort of Christmas present for the worthy people who, in the interim, have loyally supported a handful of socialist dictators' (1961: 77). Rather, she says, 'it begins simultaneously with the beginnings of the destruction of class rule and of the construction of socialism' (1961: 77). Luxemburg's great insight is to see the need for democracy *within* revolution not just *after* it. But with her very next sentence – that this requires 'seizure of power by the socialist party' and 'the dictatorship of the proletariat' (1961: 77) – she gambles away the very thing she seemed to have won. So to say, Luxemburg sees through Lenin's instrumental reasoning but is unable to discard his hierarchical and state-oriented thought.

For Lenin and his followers, the issue of prefiguration – implicit in Luxemburg's comments on a democratic revolution beginning here and now – was non-existent. The only question about 'organization' to be considered was how revolution might maximize the resources (the personnel) that it had to hand. The concept of prefiguration, by contrast, raises a whole host of wider and deeper questions, not least about exactly how present struggles (or modes of struggle) relate to a future of an emancipated kind. What is absent in Leninism is the realization that, for example, a military struggle tends to project a military future, just as a social democratic struggle which turns on gaining state power tends to call up a future where maintaining state power becomes an end in itself. The 'iron law of oligarchy' tends to crush even the best intentions of Communist Party activists.

Today's struggles break dramatically with the parameters of Leninism. Their focus on prefiguration equips them uniquely to go beyond Leninism's instrumental and institutional legacy.[1] In today's 'movement of the squares' (which unites movements in the global south with the Arab Spring, Occupy, the Indignados, Nuit Debout and a host of movements since), 'horizontality' (see Graeber 2013: 89–90) and unconstrained discussion (Graeber 2013: 141–2) are not merely 'tactics' which may or might not prove efficacious, they are part of struggle's emancipatory aim.[2] In the Occupy movement of 2011–13, for instance, recognition was a central issue. For the crowd insurgencies and the Occupations of the post-2011 period, 'horizontality' was not just a tactical method; it was, in David Graeber's words, the 'essence of what we were trying to do' (2013: 141). What Graeber calls 'horizontality' and what we understand by mutual recognition – that is, mutual recognition in a *Phenomenology*-style sense – are one and the same. When John Holloway (2016: 11) equates emancipation with 'the mutual recognition of dignities', he is thinking along similar lines. Not the least of Occupy's claims to attention is that, unusually among left-wing movements, it made mutual recognition both a means and a goal of struggle.

The prefiguration practised in today's anti-capitalism is simultaneously an end and a means – it closes the gap between the goal of revolution and the tactics used to achieve it; no conceptual space is present into which instrumental reasoning can be inserted. Common to today's anti-capitalist struggles is that they not only refuse an unjust, unfree and unsustainable social world but also attempt – through their forms of participation, organization and ways of thinking – to bring into existence an entirely new one. In the various occupations of public and private space, in the development of 'consensus' forms of decision-making, in the experiments with not-for-profit education, in the various mutualist networks set up as alternatives to austerity, in the action of rescuing and giving homes to refugees, individuals in these struggles not only say 'no' to an unfree, unequal and exploitative form of life but also develop among themselves social relations of equality, democracy and freedom. In these actions it is as if the desired future of self-determination can – in however marginalized and interstitial form – exist in the here and now. Today's struggles dismantle contradictory forms of recognition in the same act as they build the mutual recognition that is their global social ideal.

A reader can begin to see where the theory of this book – the history of the idea of recognition – and practice flow together. Recent uprisings exemplify, in our opinion, what we have pointed to in Hegel's and Marx's thinking: contradicted and alienated recognition striving to become mutual recognition. However tentative and marginal, the new politics visible in Occupy and post-Occupy movements are themselves living examples of mutually recognitive interaction, islands of mutual recognition in a hierarchical and alienated social world. In ways that have rejuvenated a Left that was hamstrung by the Leninist problem of organization and often hidebound by its focus on the white, male industrial working class, the new social movements have brought a whole new range of activists to anti-capitalist struggle, individuals previously excluded by the patriarchal and racial hierarchy of traditional Left parties.[3] The broadening of the revolutionary Left is one of the most hopeful developments of recent years.

At this point, however, a historical note is in order. The notion of prefiguration, although brought to the fore in twentieth-century feminism and Occupy, has lengthy roots. Among radicals of the seventeenth-century English Civil War period a common assumption was that a major social and spiritual change was on its way. When Gerard Winstanley's Diggers launched an experiment with communism on St George's Hill in Surrey in 1649, prefigurative thinking was at work. The Diggers' manifesto proposed to 'lay the foundation of making the earth a common treasure for all, both rich and poor. That every one that is born in the land may be fed by the earth, his mother that brought him forth' (Winstanley 1973: 84; for discussion see Linebaugh and Rediker 2013: 85–6, 141–2). When in the same period the anarchistic and blasphemous 'Ranters' spoke of a 'free community' (Coppe cited in Smith 1983: 96), they were picturing it as a realm of absolute freedom which is imminent and, so to say, already at the gate. In his *Smoke in the Temple* of 1646, the radical preacher John Saltmarsh invoked 'free debates and free conferences' held 'for all and of all sorts that will'; he hoped that 'light [will] come in at the window which cannot come in at the door' (Saltmarsh cited in Woodhouse 1992: 181). Saltmarsh's words might be applied without change to Occupy-style democracy and to revolutionary thought today. If we are to generalize this point, we might say that, unlike orthodox Marxism and its problem of organization, revolution today picks up on strands of thinking that have been dormant for centuries. It takes up a 'history from below', to use Walter Benjamin's idea (1969: 256–7), that has been missing from traditional historiography, and rids itself of the scientism of the nineteenth century. It looks once again to a 'world turned upside down' (Hill 1975) in which freedom is the key.

What these historical precursors of prefiguration tell us is that movements which 'practiced what they preached' have long been guardians of a revolutionary flame. Theirs were no mere utopian exercises but rather show ways in which social relations of freedom and equality can be built and spread in the here and now. A politics of recognition, we suggest, specifically a politics which acknowledges the revolutionary implications of Hegel's notion of mutual recognition, is therefore uniquely equipped to make sense of the current historical conjuncture and to see why it offers renewed hope for the future.

A number of political priorities follow from what we are saying. First and most importantly, is that discussion – 'horizontal', consensus-oriented discussion – has a pre-eminent place in any revolutionary movement. Mutual recognition is an inherently self-educative process. It is not surprising, therefore, that in recent occupations, the themes of prefiguration and education have emerged in tandem – alternative seminars, free universities, teach-ins and so on.

Second, and linked to this, mutual recognition is a 'forum' or an 'assembly' in which the corrosive history of hierarchies can be brought to the table and rectified. It is where the patriarchy and racial discrimination, the myriad forms of inequality and prejudice that have had such stultifying effects upon society – and upon left-wing movements – can be addressed and abolished. Mutually recognitive movements attempt to embody the very radical equality and openness to all comers that they wish to establish in society at large. I recognize others, just as they recognize me: we recognize each other as real (and not just formal) equals (here is the decisive break with liberalism). Casting aside prejudice and presumption, we begin to create the freedom and equality that we seek to establish at a global scale. Mutual recognition is the crucible into which every obstacle to freedom is thrown and out of which an emancipated social existence may be forged.

Third, because mutual recognition is by definition nothing static, nothing that can 'rest on its laurels', it is also the court of appeal in which any new charges of inequality and discrimination can be heard, in which any newly perceived inequality or discrimination or exclusion can be addressed and remedied. Mutual recognition is the self-correcting praxis of an intertwined freedom and equality. It is a self-educative movement of liberation. If mutual recognition thus understood is present in a revolutionary movement, then revolution has a future. If mutual recognition is absent, or is sacrificed to a more-or-less-distant strategic goal, the revolution risks losing its way.

Fourth, because mutual recognition begins here and now to reverse the domination of capital, it inevitably involves struggle against enclosure and the relentless spread of private property. It is no coincidence that occupiers 'reclaim the streets' from the powers of commerce and the state (and from the rule of the automobile, symbol of capital's domination of public space). It is often the residual public space in a city that offers a fortuitous site for occupation. Often the occupation itself poses the question of 'who does urban space belong to?'[4] Thus a university occupation poses a question of students, lecturers and administrators alike: What and who is educational space for? Is it for capitalist ends – doing the training work of businesses, learning to be an 'entrepreneurial self' – or is education a public good that should nurture critical minds? The spaces seized from capitalist enclosure serve in turn as a 'home' for 'struggle outwards' – to employ Yotam Marom's terms in conversation with Naomi Klein (Marom 2012).[5] Wherever a base exists in which individuals are strengthened by mutually recognitive interaction, they are emboldened to venture out and multiply these interactions, to retake capitalist space and turn it to non-capitalist ends. In revolutionary struggle, what matters above all else, and before all else, is that mutual recognition – the life and interaction in and through which freedom may be sustained – exists in a tangible and directly experiential manner.

Why – a sociologist or detached observer may ask – is sustaining freedom the be all and end all? The answer is that a revolution, if it is to count as such, must start as it intends to go on.[6] Once revolution cools the white heat of mutually recognitive interaction, a future of hierarchical and role-definitional alienation points towards a grey and grim infinity. If, by contrast, a mutually recognitive 'home' is sustained, revolution – whatever violence may be hurled against it – retains its rationale. 'Struggle outwards' remains revolutionary because the goal of revolution remains in play.

We mention here the violence hurled against mutual recognition and, in doing so, touch on a crucial theme. Is mutual recognition best understood as a pacifist practice or may it also use violence? One answer suggests itself. If revolution is to be prefigurative, if we must 'start as we intend to go on', it seems fair to say that revolutionary action should be of a non-violent kind. And indeed social movements today *are* largely non-violent: non-violent direct action is an approach with a considerable philosophy and notable successes behind it. Yet non-violence is typically met with overwhelming state force and repression. As Chomsky notes, protesters can never win an arms race with the state: 'If you take up a stick they'll come after you with a gun. You pick up a gun; they'll come after you with an assault rifle. You take an assault rifle; they'll come after you with a tank' (Chomsky 2016). Gunn's and Wilding's sympathies lie with non-violence – but there is a complication that should be noted. In a number of cases, radicals who favour non-violence against persons do so because they view human life as sacred or sacrosanct. If they are to be consistent, such radicals must base their position on theism and/or on a notion of human rights. We, for ourselves, do not invoke a deity. And, as readers familiar with Marx's critique of rights (Marx and Engels 1975a: 162–5), we are reluctant to place our hopes in those same human rights or the institutions that claim to protect them.[7] Instead, our sympathy for non-violent action is based on prefiguration. If one's goal is to further mutual recognition, launching oneself in the opposite direction is a problematic course. Means are, so to say, *ends in the making* and humane ends rarely follow from inhumane means. Death, Hegel tells us, destroys the very possibility of mutual recognition (1977: 114–15); it cannot become mutual recognition's means without falling into contradiction.[8]

The violent suppression of experiments in mutual recognition is not the only way in which such experiments can end – or be ended. Another is through co-optation. In an all-too-familiar scenario, the state summons 'the leaders' of a revolutionary movement for negotiations and by offering them power-sharing and concessions they are persuaded to enter government: the movement is incorporated into the traditional political institutions, its goals diluted and its members sold out. In his survey of Latin American politics, Benjamin Dangl (2010) refers to a 'dance' that goes forward between states and social movements of an amorphous or horizontal sort. Dangl's title – *Dancing with Dynamite* – indicates how fatal to grassroots movements the dance can be. Death in the dance is not the sudden repression of a movement but slow suffocation through statification or institutionalization.

In other cases, the co-optation of social movements is a result of an understandable exhaustion. It is a commonplace of theories of social movements that they rise and fall, become active and dormant, often because of the sheer amount of energy and time that struggle against a powerful opponent takes.[9] How can mutual recognition be sustained in such circumstances? How can real democracy survive when it requires time and energy and may take for granted the ability and willingness of individuals and their families to participate and support? This is a question that any revolutionary must address and which no theory of revolution grounded in recognition may avoid.

Our response to this – very real problem – is as follows. For any notion of mutual recognition to be practically realistic it must be acknowledged that in the course of their lives, humans pass through a range of situations and circumstances. Typically, the human life-process follows a path from infancy to old age, one that involves periods of health and illness, personal independence and family commitments. A picture of mutually recognitive society remains superficial unless it is viewed as a place where each of these life stages form the ever-present background. Mutual recognition must be imagined as going forward in a society where each of these situations may represent a hurdle to full political participation. Who holds the baby while a political point is being made? How may a disabled or bedridden individual participate in a meeting? Such questions are swept under the carpet by the traditional Left and its 'problem of organization'. Yet answers to these questions must be found if mutual recognition is not to be truncated or exclusive. Whatever the specific answer is, whatever technical solutions may be found, mutual recognition must itself be the guiding principle. Who holds the baby? No gender inequality or role definition may prescribe the answer. May a disabled person participate equally? No human falls outside recognition's realm. Should the wisdom of age outweigh the views of the young? Traditional authority has no place in a mutually recognitive world.

Participation – its preconditions, its nature, its quantitative and qualitative extent – must itself be at issue in the exercise of real democracy. This was why the early debates in the Occupy uprisings of 2011–13 were so lengthy (and why they sometimes tested the patience of even enthusiastic supporters[10]): they were democratic debates over the very definition of democracy. To those who wanted instant political action such debates could appear wearisome and indulgent, yet without them any movement falls back on the traditional divide between cadre (those issuing orders) and rank and file (those acting on orders). Occupy and other movements of direct democracy break fundamentally with this elitism; they live by the principles that 'everyone should have equal say (call this "equality"), and nobody should be compelled to do anything they really don't want to do (call this "freedom")' (Graeber n.d.). When one takes on board this fundamental and momentous premise, there is no turning back to the traditional Left. There is no short circuit to political action.[11]

The high-profile eviction of Occupy from Zuccotti Park, Taksim Square and St Paul's London resulted not from some internal failure of horizontalism but from the violent power of frightened states. The squares were still full of determined activists when they were cleared by batons, water cannon and tear gas. In this sense it is entirely wrong – as one pessimistic strain in left-wing writing has it – to speak of Occupy's 'defeat'. Sure enough, soon after these evictions, Occupy-style protests reappeared in other parts of the world (France's Nuit Debout, America's Black Lives Matter, Hong Kong's Umbrella protest, Greece's Aganaktismenoi which set up mutual aid for victims of austerity, the municipalist movement in Spain, Germany's Ende Gelände which seeks an immediate end to fossil fuel extraction), showing that leaderless movements have become the norm. Something in left-wing politics has changed and will not be undone. That the chemistry of revolution has altered is visible in the very dynamism of these movements – the fact that when they fail to live up the promise of horizontal organization or when 'gurus' try to take power, internal struggles begin that push for democratization. Today's activists are wise to the poison of oligarchy and will not be fooled by the old elitism.

Commoning and the problem of scale

We have discussed the 'horizontal' and directly democratic struggles of recent years as living examples of mutual recognition. Is this the only example of mutual recognition in practice we could give? By no means. A further example is to be found in the notion – increasingly influential in left-wing thinking today – of *the commons*. What exactly is meant by the commons? Left-wing thinkers of the commons make a contrast between commoning (or what they sometimes term 'communalizing' or 'commonizing') and communism in the traditional sense (see, for example, Thompson 1993, Sitrin 2012, Wall 2014, Bollier and Helfrich 2015, Holloway 2016, De Angelis 2017, Federici 2019). What is the difference between the commons and communism? The chief distinction is that, over the years of the Soviet Union's existence, communism (and socialism) became synonymous with an arrangement where property is owned by the state. According to Engels (1959: 387), during the communist era, the state 'withers away'. Before this can occur, however, the revolutionary goal is to ensure state ownership of whatever property a society may possess. To employ the terminology of natural law theory, state ownership is an instance of the 'positive community of things' (see S. Pufendorf 1934: Book IV, chapter IV). By contrast, where a notion of a *commons* is concerned, there is no mention of statehood. As the historian E. P. Thompson makes clear (1993: Ch. III), the question of who had access to a common could be fiercely disputed but, this said, arrangements concerning a commons might be informal. Who was to look after common land? In historical terms what we could call a 'common sense of the commons' was widespread which largely protected it from overuse. Viewed in this light, Garret Hardin's notorious 'tragedy of the commons' (Hardin 1968) refers not to some natural tendency but to a historical exception, where enclosure has occurred and possessive individualism becomes rife. By contrast, a common as understood by left-wing thinkers is a range of resources that may be accessed freely and which are shared and employed at no cost. The use concerned is cooperative and sustainable. Commoning's products are goods but not commodities.

How does this relate to mutual recognition? Our answer is that the two are deeply intertwined. To engage in commoning involves a unique form of interaction. It involves recognizing the other as someone with specific needs and equal claims upon common resources. Commoning entails recognizing both the particularity and the universality of other humans. It admits that the needs of the other will be diverse but holds that these are best met by holding goods in common and sharing them according to need. The uniqueness of other individuals is recognized in my attention to their specific needs – this a state cannot do, oriented as it is to typical needs at the scale of national populations. The state can, as it were, recognize universality but not particularity; it leaves out of account an essential aspect of human being. Only commoning – as opposed to communism understood in the sense of state management of production – can achieve the recognition of our universality *and* our particularity.

Just as commoning contrasts with state planning, so it stands opposed to market exchange. In market exchange, I seek to satisfy my needs by acquiring the other's commodity, just as they seek to satisfy their needs by acquiring mine (or my money – the abstract equivalent). As Adam Smith famously described it, in such a transaction 'it is not from the benevolence of the butcher, the brewer, or the baker that we expect our dinner, but from their regard to their own self-interest. We address ourselves not to their humanity but to their self-love, and never talk to them of our own necessities, but of their advantages' (1979: 27). Self-interest, in other words, is the market's irrefragable logic. What recognition exists in market exchange is the minimal formal recognition between egoists. In a market, to take an interest in the other's well-being would, as Smith's words show, be irrational. Commoning could not be more different to this egoistic logic. It is a deeply recognitive process. It renders *egoism* irrational (since self-interested exploitation of a commons is contradictory and unsustainable). It encourages concern (the very 'benevolence' mocked by Smith) for the other and a realization of human interdependence, just as it provides a justification for democratic decision-making about the commons itself. Commoning is a mode of production where each individual exists cooperatively *through* others, not *in spite of* others.[12]

Massimo de Angelis has noted the internal relation between commoning and horizontalism. Decision-making on what a commons produces and distributes, he suggests, can only consistently be made in a directly democratic and non-hierarchical way. This entails, he says, cultivating 'a continuous flux of argument and a diversity of beliefs and values, but with a mechanism that is able to reach consensual decisions' (De Angelis 2017: xiii). Commoning is, in De Angelis's words, 'an ongoing dance of values, kept together by the rhythm of our daily reproduction and the decisions that need to be communally taken in given contexts' (De Angelis 2017, see also 104, 231). In this vivid description De Angelis points, implicitly, to mutual recognition.

Alongside De Angelis, Silvia Federici is another present-day theorist who restores the commons to its rightful place at the centre of left-wing theory and practice. Commoning is a theme that runs throughout her writing and she writes movingly and thoughtfully on it. And when she says that there is 'no commons without community' (Federici 2019: 110) she is adamant that 'community' must be understood 'not as a gated reality, a grouping of people joined by exclusive interests of religion or ethnicity, but rather as a quality of relations, a principle of cooperation and of responsibility to each other and to the earth, the forests, the seas, the animals' (Federici 2019). In a number of recent articles, Federici has emerged as one of neoliberalism's most trenchant critics. She points, for instance, to the land grab that has been a key aspect of neoliberal policies in the global south. Against a background of 'commercialisation of agriculture' and 'loss of communal land' (2019: 120), the 'figure of the worker' has, in metropolitan countries, turned into that of 'the migrant, the itinerant, the refugee' (2019: 22). The international sweep of Federici's thought is salutary, as European politics has sunk into the self-importance of local and domestic themes. In Marxist terms, it is time at last to give to 'the proletariat' a genuinely international sense. The stereotypical figure of 'the proletarian' in leftist thinking is burly and bewhiskered – and white and male. Federici leaves us in no doubt that this must change.[13]

For Federici and a number of other writers, the analysis of capital's (often violent) attempt to dispossess and privatize the commons raises an important issue in Marxist theory. Towards the end of *Capital* Volume One, Marx refers to 'primitive accumulation' which, he says, 'precedes capitalist accumulation' and is its 'point of departure' (Marx 1976: 873). How should 'primitive accumulation' be understood?

Traditionally, primitive accumulation has been pictured as going forward in a specific period (say, the sixteenth and seventeenth centuries) – as, perhaps, the words just quoted from Marx seem to imply. For Werner Bonefeld, however, primitive accumulation takes place in an ongoing fashion throughout the capitalist period. There is, we consider, a sense in which Bonefeld must be right on this: when Marx speaks of 'primitive accumulation' he is not picturing the growth of figures on a bank balance but, more crucially, of a social process where workers are prised away from their means of subsistence and have no alternative but to sell their labour power if they are to survive. Elsewhere, Marx makes the point explicit (1976: 874). There is a danger that, unless the working class is continually prised away from its means of subsistence, capitalism's workforce will either wither away or assert its autonomy, as Marx's example of 'the unhappy Mr Peel' deserted by his workers shows (1976: 932–3). This may be so but, before passing on from the controversy which involves Bonefeld, we would like to note a political issue at stake. Was there a period, some centuries ago, when capitalism relied on coercion and violence? And has there been a subsequent period when, relying on the 'silent compulsion of economic relations' (Marx 1976: 899), capitalism presents a more civilized face? For Bonefeld, as for ourselves, the historical issue is not clear-cut. What is clear-cut is the contradiction to the worker's autonomy that obtains for as long as capitalism exists.

To the present brief list of thinkers whose ideas chime with our own, we should like to add Raúl Zibechi. Like Federici, Zibechi is a recent theorist who helps us to understand the commons and struggles to preserve it against capitalist incursion. Zibechi's *Territories in Resistance* (2012: 20) points to the 'new world' that is being born in the 'gaps that are opening up in capitalism'. Commons are an instance of 'gaps' in this sense. The international 'movement of the squares' of recent times is another. We note, for instance, that the slogan of the municipalist movement in Spain (a movement which draws on anarchist and direct-democratic ideas) is 'Ahora en Común' (Now in Common), alluding both to commoning and common action but also to the urgency of beginning *now* as we mean to go on (Rubio-Pueyo 2017: 4). The point of revolutionary struggle today is to multiply these gaps until they join up and the commons becomes global – we push out capital from our lives to the extent that we multiply, extend and enrich the commons.

But how, a reader may well ask, does a politics of mutual recognition understood in this way – as a practice of unconstrained, inclusive conversation or as a practice of commoning – address questions of political action that may require force or that must be addressed at a global level? Perhaps the most persuasive critic of our position is David Harvey in his book *Rebel Cities*, and a response to Harvey is in order here. Harvey shows sympathy for the outbreak of struggles that began in 2010 but objects to the organizational form these take. Lamenting that the term 'hierarchy' is 'virulently unpopular with much of the left these days' – and that 'only horizontalism' is seen as 'politically correct' – he suggests that this development allows important issues to be 'evaded' (Harvey 2013: 69). What issues are being evaded? In part, what is at stake here is that Harvey judges a form of organization or political initiative in terms quite different to our own: his criteria for assessing a struggle are its 'demands' (Harvey 2013: xiv, 22) or its tendency to promote a specific goal (2013: 136).[14] When he comments on the horizontal political discussion that is a key part of Occupy and evaluates its merit or demerit as a 'tactic', his book reveals its indebtedness to the Marxist–Leninist 'problem of organization' – and the instrumentalist discourse of means and ends that prevailed there. He passes over in virtual silence the novelty of Occupy and its gift to the radical Left. As in the tradition of Marxism–Leninism, Harvey takes the goal of struggle to be one which a theorist may know before struggle is embarked upon: there can be no question of evaluating a movement in terms of its self-education or in terms of the goals or aims which it, itself, evolves. Under the sway of 'the problem of organization', nothing which fails to promote the instrumental goal in an efficient fashion is seen as having political value.

The most important flaw Harvey finds in current struggles is, he says, its failure to address the need for *global* political action. What he calls the Left's current 'fetishism of pure horizontality' means that it is unable to deal with issues whose scale – so he argues – requires 'hierarchical' forms of organization (2013:). The large-scale problems that *Rebel Cities* has in mind include 'how one organizes a whole city' (2013: 152), how one organizes a 'metropolitan region as a whole' (2013: 80) and – more ambitiously still – how one tackles global warming (2013: 69).

Why should such large-scale issues require a hierarchical mode of organization? Harvey's answer to this question becomes clear when he considers Elinor Ostrom's work on the commons and commoning.[15] A key finding in Ostrom's research is that the famed 'tragedy of the commons' need not occur if users of the commons are allowed to interact (instead of being seen as isolated agents as on Rational Choice theory). So to say, Ostrom bears out Thompson's observation – directed against Hardin – that commoners are 'not without common-sense' (Thompson 1993: 107; for discussion, see Wall 2014: Ch. 1). The difficulty which Harvey finds with Ostrom is that, as she admits, any large-scale issue 'requires a "nested" structure of decision-making' (Harvey 2013: 69) – and 'nesting' brings into play 'leadership structures alongside egalitarian assemblies' (Harvey 2013: 150). It brings into play 'some higher-order hierarchical structure' and Ostrom is 'naive' to believe that 'strong hierarchical constraints and active enforcement' are dispensable (Harvey 2013: 84). In short, face-to-face informality is insufficient; for 'nested' face-to-face situations to be combined, and for issues common to them to be handled equitably, there must be overarching rules of the game. Decisions about specifics must be subordinated to decisions about generalities. Authority must have layers. The further one moves from a local focus, the more evidently a need for 'hierarchy' is seen.

How might the horizontalism we have set out in this chapter be defended against the charge that hierarchy ('verticality') is needed if large-scale issues such as climate change and international justice are to be addressed? A first response might be to argue that many issues that, conventionally, call for centralization may in fact be approached in a decentred or non-hierarchical way. So to say, large-scale issues raise no distinctive problems and might be addressed by what Zibechi (2010: 51) terms 'rhizomatic' (i.e. non-centralized) means. Does this solve all of the problems that Harvey points to? We admit that on its own this argument is unlikely to satisfy Harvey or his followers.

But a further and more persuasive response to Harvey's challenge may be proposed. Our proposal, not surprisingly, turns on the notion of mutual recognition. In our view, mutual recognition is not merely one form of organization among others. It is not merely a form or pattern or practice of interaction which may be assessed – and, if necessary, set aside – in the light of its capacity to further an externally given objective. On the contrary, mutual recognition is the *mode in which emancipated social relations exist*. If mutual recognition is a sine qua non of emancipation, it is at the same time a condition of the flexibility which – we suggest – a democratic handling of large-scale issues requires. Where mutual recognition exists as a living principle, a range of organizational patterns or tactics may be employed – and selected as of need. Tactics can be selected without hardening into a fixed set of strategies or doctrines, just as an organizational form can be adopted without congealing into a political structure. An international form of organization can be taken up, for instance, but only because a mutually recognitive community decides upon it – this decision can be revoked, for instance, if hierarchies arise or if the organization ceases to act democratically. Through its very *flexibility*, we propose, a mutually recognitive community can address problems of 'scale'. For the 'problem of organization' (within whose confines Harvey's discussion moves) such flexibility is not – and, owing to its instrumentalism, cannot be – available.

On our approach, the distinctive character of large-scale issues is admitted: problems of climate change and social justice are seen as reaching beyond the confines of any single community. But (we claim) participatory democracy is not tied to local or relatively small-scale or face-to-face issues. Its range may be extended: society-wide questions can be addressed in a participatory way.

For the problem of 'scale' to be surmounted, a flexible attitude to organization, along the lines we propose, is required. According to such an attitude, local issues and society-wide issues may be addressed in a way that is effective and appropriate, that is, flexibly. Second, however – and this 'second' is vitally important – the flexibility that we have in mind is conceivable only if mutual recognition exists. If mutual recognition exists and is flourishing, emancipation (and the 'educative' self-transformation that emancipation entails) is present. A community may safely undertake instrumental action as long as its (non-instrumental) values and underlying principles are secure. If mutual recognition is absent, and if a culture of mutual recognition fails to inform all social actions, then instrumental thinking and action become endemic and an emancipatory project (however well intentioned) becomes a self-defeating morass. Discipline and hierarchy all too easily become not just means but ends: they harden into social institutions and structures, just as undemocratic actions calcify into behaviour and character. If mutual recognition is absent from the outset of revolution, there is scant chance that it will emerge. By contrast, where mutual recognition is present, there is widespread (indeed, universal) awareness of fundamental social values. Such values – among them, the values of unconstrained interaction and self-determination – are everywhere and everywhen at stake. Mutually recognitive interaction is, so to say, a conversation which brings a wide range of possible circumstances and responses into play. Such a conversation is 'a permanent process of self-education' (Zibechi). It contains a dynamic that is self-sustaining.

To repeat, our position does not rule out that mutually recognitive polities may opt temporarily to take on a hierarchical structure so as to engage in a particular task. What it does deny is that hierarchical organization may become (so to say) user-friendly and benign. On the contrary, hierarchical organization is intrinsically tied to alienated (and thereby contradictory) recognition. Viewed in terms of recognition, hierarchy is damaging per se. Non-alienated or, so to say, non-toxic hierarchy is an impossibility – hierarchy remains toxic even if (for reasons of circumstance or emergency) a mutually recognitive community selects it. What we are proposing is that in a situation of mutual recognition, the toxic material of hierarchy may be handled – if not with impunity, at least in a manner that allows emancipation to survive. If emancipation survives, it is not because hierarchy has become benign. It is because mutual recognition remains the overarching principle to which organizational issues must answer. Centralized organization (which, in a given instance, mutual recognition may select) can temporarily be chosen because it involves trust – and trust, like 'forgiveness' (Hegel 1977: 407), presupposes mutual recognition. Where mutual recognition obtains, interaction resembles a sea upon which islands of hierarchy may or may not appear. Even if these islands become massive, the sea which surrounds them is one where unstructured interaction prevails. It is in this light that an alternative to the Marxist–Leninist 'problem of organization' may be posed. Any revolutionary movement which loses sight of mutual recognition loses its raison d'être. More, mutual recognition is not merely one version of struggle among others – but an unconditional priority which must regulate political action at every step.[16]

For the 'problem of organization', as (seemingly) for Harvey, no feature of struggle can have value in this unconditional sense. A Marxist–Leninist understanding of the 'problem of organization' must exclude the notion of prefiguration or prolepsis we are setting forth: instrumental thinking forbids weaving together political means and political ends. Yet on such a view, Marx's description of communism as 'the real movement which abolishes the present state of things' (1976a, p. 49) becomes meaningless – or ill-formulated at best. In Harvey's *Rebel Cities*, we note finally, there is a silence not merely about recognition but about prolepsis (to which, for Occupy, mutual recognition is closely linked) that suggests instrumental thinking has been taken for granted. To repeat, much in *Rebel Cities* strikes us as intriguing and sympathetic. But an unreconstructed instrumentalism inherited from orthodox Marxism casts a shadow at every turn.[17]

A reader who has followed our discussion thus far may be inclined to ask, what sort of revolutionary movement may count as 'non-instrumental' in the above sense? Our answer is a 'non-instrumental' movement may be pictured as one which is self-transformative and self-educative in Zibechi's sense. For such a movement, the mutual recognition which prefigures a new world enables learning; at the same time, as participants in Occupied zones or 'territories in resistance' or a commons are the first to acknowledge, it is something to be learned. Zibechi's writings (e.g. 2010: 84–5, 2012: 87) in a sense bring us full circle, back to the work of Rosa Luxemburg. But crucially Zibechi distances himself from Luxemburg's understanding of 'spontaenity' that appeared to be the antidote to Leninism. Zibechi's insight is that class consciousness is a learning curve on the part of those in struggle, not something that arises in an 'instinctive' or 'incalculable' way (Luxemburg 2004: 193, 328) or has to be taught 'from without' (Lenin 1969: 98). Our view is that the notion of spontaneity succeeds in breaking with instrumentalist thinking if, and only if, social movements are seen, as Zibechi sees them, in a self-educative and self-transformative way.

It is tempting to say more – much more – about mutual recognition in practice. Yet the very subject matter requires that we resist this temptation. The future to which Gunn and Wilding point is one where mutually recognitive interaction prevails. One (not exhaustive) illustration of this might be an unconstrained conversation. By its very nature, the content of such a conversation would be hard to foretell. If a conversation were premised on the prevailing contradictory recognition, its course might be predicted: it is, for instance, because institutional channels of wealth guide newspaper editing, that opinions and news coverage may be foreseen. If, by contrast, the conversation were mutually recognitive and unbounded, prediction would be difficult. The only way to know where the conversation leads would be to follow – that is, join – the conversation itself.[18] A discussion of mutual recognition in practice would carry the warning: wait and see. Should such a discussion end on this unpromising note? Our feeling is that this is unnecessary. Rather than poring over the future, we can begin – right here and right now – to talk.

5

Recognition's environment

In the previous chapter we showed ways in which recognition is not just an idea or ideal but has practical political consequences – issues in the history of ideas have practical implications, just as practical political issues raise theoretical questions for which the history of ideas can provide answers. In particular, Hegel and Marx – understood as thinkers who share a common concern – can be touchstones for today's radical political movements. The issues of *revolutionary organization* and of *commoning* were two themes where the radical implications of Hegel's and Marx's idea of recognition became clear. We believe that a *myriad* of *further political themes* can be addressed in radical ways once recognition is brought to the table. Of course, a straightforward list of such instances would be of doubtful use. More productive would be to explore cases where the significance of recognition to a specific issue would otherwise be difficult to see. The present chapter undertakes just this task. The issue that we focus on here is that of *climate change*.

The choice of this issue is not incidental. Climate change is not simply one topic among others that the Left must address; it is arguably the most important issue facing us today. Kristin Ross has recently suggested that 'defending the conditions for life on the planet has become the new and incontrovertible horizon of meaning of all political struggle' (Ross 2018). The term 'horizon' may be misleading, however, because climate change is not simply an issue that looms ahead; it is already upon us, impacting societies around the globe in terrifying ways. 'It is worse, much worse than you think', David Wallace-Wells's book *The Uninhabitable Earth* begins, a work which draws together the latest scientific prognoses and which cannot but leave the reader in a state of dread. Existential questions which seemed outmoded are made topical once more by the course of a world history that now threatens human life itself. 'Climate change is fast', Wallace-Wells continues, 'much faster than it seems we have the capacity to recognize and acknowledge, but it is also long, almost longer than we can truly imagine' (Wallace-Wells 2018: 16). In the era of climate change the global Left's struggle against capitalism widens in scope while becoming existentially more urgent: it becomes not just an issue of freedom and justice but one of survival. To the stark choice offered by Rosa Luxemburg at the start of the twentieth century, between 'socialism and barbarism' (2004: 321) we may now add a third possibility: extinction.

In what ways can the idea of mutual recognition help us think through the enormity of the task we face in dealing with climate change? Do we meet here the limits of what a revolutionary politics of recognition can bring to the table of current issues? Or might it be that through the notion of mutual recognition the Left's cause can be reconciled with the environmental cause and 'red' and 'green' politics can flow together? Our argument in this final chapter is that the two struggles can – and must – become one.

Red and green

Famously, ecological and left-wing ideas are not easy to marry. A string of books from the 1970s and 1980s grounded their green politics on an equal rejection of both capitalism and socialism. The two axes of twentieth-century politics were for many green thinkers and politicians two sides of an overarching 'industrialism' that was destroying life on the planet. The landscapes of 'actually existing socialism' – in many respects just as polluted and depleted as those of the capitalist West – were viewed by greens as the logical outcome of Marxist thought, whose 'Promethean' confidence in the mastery of nature mirrored capitalism's ruthless pursuit of economic growth. Given the elision of Soviet Bloc economies with Marx's thinking, and the assumption that a logic of economic growth united East and West, it was perhaps unsurprising that many activists took as their inspiration the slogan of Germany's *Die Grünen*: 'neither left nor right but in front'.

At the same time, counter-tendencies were developing which sought to reconcile red and green ideas, for instance, in the writings of Marxists such as Ted Benton and Elmar Altvater, and across the Atlantic in the anarchist-inspired 'social ecology' of Murray Bookchin and the 'ecosocialism' of Joel Kovel and Michael Löwy. These thinkers showed ways in which environmental goals were far from incompatible with left-wing assumptions, and that indeed an alliance of forces was much needed. In the 1990s, the criticism of Marx as a 'Promethean' or 'productivist' was put in doubt by close readings of his work undertaken in Paul Burkett's *Marx and Nature* (1999) and John Bellamy Foster's *Marx's Ecology* (2000). These studies found in Marx auguries of our current environmental predicament and brought to light his prophetic notion of a 'metabolic interaction between man and the earth' that capitalism has 'disturbed' (Marx 1976: 638).

The recent publication of the 'Ecological Notebooks' from Marx's final years give renewed cause to rethink long-standing assumptions about Marxism and the environment. These notebooks reveal that, before his death, Marx was taking increasing interest in environmental ideas, particularly in then-current scientific theories of chemistry and agriculture which indicated a looming crisis in the global fertility of soil, a trend he seems to have believed might be as significant as the 'economic' crises inherent in capital. Kohei Saito's research on these notebooks, discussed in his recent *Karl Marx's Ecosocialism* (2019), shows Marx would likely have given ecological crises and the 'metabolism' they disrupt a more central role in the second edition of *Capital*. Marx's letter to Engels of February 1866 gives a sense of the seismic shift in the critique of political economy this would have involved: 'I have been going to the Museum [the British Library] in the day-time and writing at night. I had to plough through the new agricultural chemistry in Germany, in particularly Liebig and Schönbein, which is more important ... than all the economists put together' (Marx and Engels 1987b: 227).

These fascinating textual discoveries suggest one way in which red and green issues may be allied and that Left and ecological priorities are far from incompatible. They show that Marx's critique of capital targets not only its domination of labour but also its domination of nature, both of which Marx understood to be unsustainable. If we interpret his preoccupation with 'the fertility of the soil' as an archetype of ecological sustainability, then we can see – without too much extrapolation – Marx as having something to tell us about what today is called 'the Earth System': the interdependence of a global set of climate-determining ecosystems. Marx, so recent scholarship suggests, can justifiably be regarded not just as a 'red' but also – albeit in germinal form – as a 'green' thinker.

Previously, we mentioned that an alliance of red and green thinking had also been the focus of 'social ecology', a thinking associated with Murray Bookchin, Janet Biehl and Dan Chodorkoff. Social ecology is particularly relevant to our discussion because there one finds ecology discussed not only in left-wing terms but also implicitly in terms of recognition. For social ecology, the history of humans' destructive relationship to the natural world is seen to stem from *hierarchies within society*. Humans' domination of nature is a concomitant of domination of human by human (Bookchin 1980: 75–6). Bookchin was a reader of Hegel, Marx and the critical theory tradition and so it is not surprising that here green thought sees something of the radical implications of Left Hegelianism. Because hierarchies are, in our terminology, instances of *one-sided and unequal recognition*, social ecology offers a critical diagnosis that in many ways parallels our own.

Social ecology has seen a renaissance in recent years. It has also, we note, had practical political effects. Reading Bookchin's work, in particular, was the catalyst for Abdullah Öcalan to turn the Kurdish PKK from a patriarchal Leninist party into a non-hierarchical ecofeminist movement. Imprisoned by the Turkish government in 1998, Öcalan read Bookchin's *The Ecology of Freedom* and decided to translate its Hegelian–Marxist critique of domination into practice, developing an assembly-based 'libertarian municipalism' in which women and men would have equal place. Despite military attack by Syria, Turkey, Russia and the United States, along with the brutal terrorism of ISIS, the Kurds in Rojava have repeatedly defended their experiment in non-hierarchical social existence (see Öcalan 2011, 2019 and the foreword by Holloway in the latter volume).[1]

If, as social ecology argues, it is hierarchy between humans – above all in the systematized domination that is capitalism – that lies at the root of the environmental crisis, then one influential explanation of our predicament – so-called deep ecology – is to be abandoned. Deep ecology lays the blame for the destruction of the environment at the feet of human hubris and 'speciesism' (see Singer 2011: Ch. 3). Humans, so deep ecologists argue, fail to appreciate their equality with other beings in the web of life. Bookchin saw early on that the 'deep ecological' line of thought is misguided and perilous: the charge of 'speciesism' overlooks the real culprits of our environmental predicament. Blaming abstractions such as 'humanity' or 'Homo sapiens' conceals, in Bookchin's words, 'vast differences, often bitter antagonisms, that exist between privileged whites and people of colour, men and women, rich and poor, oppressor and oppressed' (1993). The same error occurs when the culprit is taken to be 'society' or 'civilization', terms that obscure the differences 'between free, nonhierarchical, class, and stateless societies on the one hand, and others that are, in varying degrees, hierarchical, class-ridden, statist, and authoritarian' (1993).

Deep ecology's error, one may add, reflects a tendency of green politics more generally: it often blames world views and philosophies, as though changing these alone would create a society in harmony with nature. Green politics typically lacks an analysis of the anti-ecological dynamic of capitalism, a dynamic which compels people – often against their better judgement or their higher principles – into unsustainable relationships with the natural world. To this extent, quibbling with capital about its values is to tilt at windmills. Green thinking often displays no more than a superficial understanding of capitalism, typically censuring one moment (consumption) in isolation from others (production and exchange). When consumption patterns are blamed for the climate crisis, these are detached from their role in a wider circuit of accumulation. As Marx tells us, commodities are not produced in order to be consumed (for their 'use value') but to create profit ('value'); to the capitalist their consumption and the waste this generates are mere afterthoughts. Political economy, the legitimizing science of capitalism, can only regard the natural world as an 'externality', a free resource which has no price and its degradation no cost. Already in the famous M-C-M', which Marx identified as the formula of capitalism's 'unmeasured drive for self-valorization' (1976: 377), the dynamic of environmental catastrophe is latent. On a finite planet it is a deadly reckoning.

This is where the critique of domination, the idea central to social ecology, that Bookchin developed out of a reading of Hegel, can help overcome the abstractness of green thinking and bring green and red rationales together. On the basis of the critique of domination, of 'mastery' and 'slavery' in their various historical forms, it is possible to conceive a confluence of left-wing and ecological struggles. Our suggestion is that a history of human hierarchy and coercion – in Hegelian terms, of one-sided and unequal recognition – is behind our destructive relationship to nature.[2] Capitalism, with its environmentally destructive logic, is the latest stage in a long history of the domination of human by human: a domination that now eats away at the very fabric of the Earth System.

Andreas Malm in his 2016 book *Fossil Capital: The Rise of Steam Power and the Roots of Global Warming* presents historical evidence that supports this thesis. He explores the interesting historical circumstance that the replacement of water power by steam power (from the mechanized burning of coal) can be linked directly to the domination exerted by capital over workers. The long years of enclosure and dispossession in seventeenth- to nineteenth-century England created a new class of expropriated 'freemen' who were 'unencumbered by any means of production of their own' (as Marx sardonically puts it (1976: 874)). This new class concentrated in cities where they became dependent on waged labour. The relatively autonomous cottage industry of old and which relied on water power could then be rendered uncompetitive by coal-fired machinery, and early industrialists could break one set of class relations for a more autocratic one (Malm 2016: 363–4). Coal was not cheaper than water – its success cannot be explained in economic terms. The adoption of coal-fired machinery only makes sense once we realize that it aided the capitalist in disciplining the emergent urban working class. What capital viewed as 'the annoying idiosyncrasies of human workers' could be ironed out 'by installing ever more machinery impelled by ever more powerful steam engines' (Malm 2016: 10). It is through domination that the 'fossil economy' was born: 'a socio-ecological structure, in which a certain economic process and a certain form of energy are welded together' (Malm 2016: 22). Today, 'fossil capital' seeps into almost every corner of our lives, making it hard to imagine a world without it. Yet it has a history, one that was never predestined by a logic of technological innovation but by class struggle and the specific balance of class power (Malm 2016: 335–6).

If domination is the essence of a 'fossil capitalism' that is now altering the Earth System then – contra deep ecology – no abstract 'humanity' is the root cause of environmental destruction. That destruction is the result of definite social relations existing in particular geographical and historical settings. We should really treat the 'anthropos' of the term 'anthropogenic climate change' and the now widely used periodization 'Anthropocene' as concealing what Marx calls 'the ensemble of social relations' (1992: 423).[3] If Marx points to the unsustainability of capital's 'metabolism' with the planet, he also shows us that we need to disaggregate the abstractions 'humanity' or 'society', today often taken uncritically as the cause of the ecological crisis (cf. Wilding 2008).

Whatever we term the present era – and the political stakes of terminology are considerable – its arrival is an event that potentially alters left-wing politics utterly. It invalidates, for instance, the more Promethean dreams of a Left which dreamt of economic growth put to socialist ends and of capitalist inventions rendered benign and beneficial.[4] Economic forecasts now suggest the 'business-as-usual' scenario of CO_2 emissions could lead to an economic contraction that would dwarf the

Great Depression: 'first, by producing a global economic stagnation that will play, in some areas, like a breath-taking and permanent recession; and second, by punishing the poor much more dramatically than the rich, both globally and within particular polities, showcasing an increasingly stark income inequality, unconscionable already to more and more' (Wallace-Wells 2018: 148). For decades, neoliberals have justified inequality by pointing to the benefits (even if only those that 'trickle down') of economic growth. Such founding myths would lose any residual credibility. While the Left has much to teach ecology, ecology rightly teaches the Left that infinite growth is impossible on a finite planet and that there may well be no technological fixes for social and environmental problems.

That the political field has changed utterly is something that many on the Left are reluctant to accept. Yet looking back into the Left's own intellectual history is to see the issue of environmental destruction foreshadowed. In Marx's time, as we have seen, the problems posed by declining fertility of land could be glimpsed. In the twentieth century, particularly in times of war, capital's destructive ecological trajectory became clearer still. Already in 1948 the Dutch anarchist Anton Pannekoek could suggest that 'capitalist society with its mighty technical and its entirely inadequate spiritual and moral powers' is like a 'powerful racing car with a baby at the wheel'. The car is now 'steering downright towards the abyss' (Pannekoek 1948: 20–1). Around the same time, Horkheimer and Adorno conjectured that, were capital's 'racket in nature' to continue, 'either the human species will tear itself to pieces or it will take all the earth's fauna and flora down with it, and if the earth is still young enough, the whole procedure [of evolution] will have to start again on a much lower level' (2002: 186).[5]

These prognoses come, of course, from a time before climate change was fully comprehended. Yet something in them seems uncannily prophetic. In a situation where history not so much reaches the telos of a struggle for mutual recognition as reverts to a pre-historical struggle for survival, the dream of creating a humane world would become idle.[6] An uninhabitable or barely inhabitable earth sounds like a worst-case scenario, yet recent years have shown the worst-case 'tails' of the bell curve of climate probability moving ever closer to the median. Of course a large degree of uncertainty operates in climate prediction, but uncertainty is not necessarily a friend, particularly in scenarios where feedback loops – exponential rather than linear trends – operate. This has political ramifications: enormous ones. For the Left, the danger is that our window of opportunity to overthrow capital narrows. 'The point of too late', Malm observes, 'is coming closer by the day' (2016: 20). Starkly put, the danger is that capital may scorch the earth to such a degree that a social existence built on mutual recognition becomes very difficult. If there is a hope that can be set against this possibility it is a counterfactual one, a demand that we act now on the very basis of our uncertainty about the future, in the hope against hope that it is not too late.

Worst-case ecological scenarios may also lead to worst-case political scenarios. Among the political dangers is one that Geoff Mann and Joel Wainwright (2018) call (in their book of the same name) *Climate Leviathan*. In their near-future portrait, climate change has legitimized a totalitarian power grab by the state, a state which then disciplines its populations in a manner akin to Hobbes's cynical political vision. For the sake of climate 'security', individuals trade in what liberty they have, going around (as in Hobbes's 'state of nature') armed or locking their doors at night, though now for fear not of robbers but of climate refugees. Climate Leviathan is, for Mann and Wainwright, an extrapolation of the current global balance of powers: the world's most powerful states 'are likely to become even more dominant through a concentration of political-economic power, military force, and energy resources' (2018: 26).[7] Yet, as the authors note, though Climate Leviathan may become 'the fundamental regulatory ideal motivating elites in the near future' it is 'neither inevitable nor invincible'. Any power grab by the 'extant hegemonic bloc' is 'threatened within by the usual burdens of any state-capitalist project divided by multiple accumulation strategies, and it is almost impossible to imagine that it will actually reverse climate change' (Mann and Wainwright 2018: 26, 34).

Certainly, the right-wing governments who hold power in most of the nations of the 'Global north' seem to be adopting such an approach. They appear to be gambling on little or nothing being done to mitigate climate change and so are mobilizing to secure the continued conditions for accumulation. Their response to the prospect of millions of climate refugees is a series of protectionist moves and the building of walls (real or bureaucratic) to keep out climate change's victims while protecting the wealthy culprits from the cost of climate breakdown.

Environmental justice as mutual recognition

Against this dark background of possibilities, what hope lies in the notion of mutual recognition? Our answer is a defiant one. It is that there is still a place – indeed a central place – for it. In fact, climate change and our acknowledgement of the finite and fragile character of the Earth System make mutual recognition between humans an even more urgent priority.

One rightly speaks today of 'environmental justice' and not just 'environmentalism' because it is increasingly clear that humans are differentially affected by capital's war on the planet. Just as there is no abstract 'anthropos' that is the cause of climate change, so there is no humanity-in-general who uniformly suffer its effects. 'Globally', as Ian Angus notes, '99 percent of weather disaster casualties are in developing countries, and 75 percent of them are women' (2016: 176). In the global north, the geography of climate (particularly heatwave) mortality is distributed along lines of income and racial segregation (2016: 176). The global south – kept for decades in a state of 'underdevelopment' by dependent relations of trade and debt with the north – now bears the brunt of the north's adventure with industrialization. As Ehrenreich points out, 'the long history of colonial-era expropriation, exploitation and theft echoes loudly in the new dispensation, in which the sectors of humanity that profited the least from industrialization suffer the most from its environmental impacts. The conditions that drive climate change have been created in one part of the world. The consequences have so far overwhelmingly been suffered in another' (2019a). With its inaction on climate change, the north effectively condemns the south for a crime it did not commit and with its border walls confines the condemned in an ever-warming prison. The erection of physical and legal barriers are inherently racist endeavours – a true 'climate apartheid' that enforces hierarchy by the most merciless means.

Resisting and overturning this *domination* which climate change deepens and widens is the goal of an 'environmental justice' movement that is now global in character. This movement – a source of hope amid all the bad news – takes specific forms in specific countries, for example, 'Standing Rock' in the United States and the Indigenous Environmental Network in Canada which attempt to halt the building of tar-sands pipelines. In Germany, Ende Gelände is a grassroots direct action movement that blocks the spread of opencast lignite mines and protects the forests and villages in their path. The campaign against fracking – the last and most dangerous throw of the dice for 'extractivist' capitalism – is now international in character and has had notable successes in Europe.

Each of these struggles faces the enormous power of a state-industrial complex that often has (violent) police protection. In Brazil, indigenous peoples are at the forefront of the campaign to protect the Amazon, the 'lungs of the planet'. But they face the violence of farmers committed to Bolsanaro's 'modernization' policy of felling rainforest for export markets in beef and soya. To these struggles we can add movements which are pro-refugee and pro-migrant, something that is intimately linked to the struggle against climate change. In the United States, a new social movement seeks to abolish the Immigration and Customs Enforcement authority (ICE) and, with it, Trump's intentionally 'hostile environment'. In the Mediterranean – 'the deadliest border on Earth' (Ehrenreich 2019b) – activists in movements such as Sea Watch and Sea-Eye (with its ship the Alan Kurdi) try to save the lives of those fleeing drought, famine and war. At the EU's outer edges, border and asylum-processing regimes are often just as hostile as in the United States, leaving charity workers and social movements to pick up the pieces of human lives (Della Porta 2017).

The environmental justice movement tells us that there is no sustainable future – either ecologically or socially – within capitalism. For the same reason there is no 'green capitalism' that is not a contradiction in terms. The very logic of profit – not just that of growth, as greens often assume – is anathema to environmental sustainability; the growth blamed by green politicians for our ills is a mere consequence of the accumulation that is capital's lifeblood. Climate change is, above all, a question of *injustice*; its solution can only lie beyond capitalism. Grasping this essential insight must be the fundament of any red–green politics, ecosocialism or eco-communism. 'The task, and it is truly hard, is to end capitalism and the nation, an outcome absent which untold species will die off, humans among them, dying in millions first at the borders and then everywhere, dying in queues chaotically ordered according to race and ethnicity, class, gender, sexuality, nationality' (Commune 2019).

For us, climate justice shows very clearly that mutual recognition is not simply an issue for the future but a question of how we act in the here and now. At one point in her recent book *No Is Not Enough*, Naomi Klein writes that 'what we are hurtling towards is the future glimpsed in New Orleans and Baghdad. A world demarcated into Green Zones and Red Zones and black sites for whoever doesn't cooperate' (Klein 2017: 180–1). If the passage from Naomi Klein may be qualified, it is by making it explicit that the world which she foresees has already come into being. This is how the rich in the developed world are already responding to climate change – by employing the well-worn acts of possessive individualists, of Hobbesian individuals who do not recognize others as fellow humans.[8] They build walls and gated communities and object to the cost of rescuing refugees. They warn of 'pull factors' for migration and do their best to create 'hostile environments' as deterrents.

There is an alternative, and that alternative is the practice of mutual recognition. It is a practice already visible in the environmental justice movement, in the actions of all those movements which recognize the very human needs of climate change's victims – movements which have welcomed refugees and which acknowledge the planet as a shared home where borders have no place. Indeed the slogan 'Refugees Welcome!' is, we suggest, *recognitive* – it recognizes a common humanity and particular need in the other.[9] When seen as a practice of recognition, the hospitality of declaring 'Refugees Welcome!' appears not as simple largesse but as acknowledgement of human interdependence; it returns to the other a self-determination of which circumstances have deprived them. If climate change is already upon us, anti-capitalist struggle is not just a means to an end of an ecological society; we can and must begin to build the ecological society – the mutually recognitive society – in the here and now. Just as democracy serves the Occupy movement as a prefiguration – as the reality and goal of struggle – so ecological struggle begins today in the protection of ecosystems, the defence and expansion of the commons, and a hospitality towards the suffering peoples of the earth.

Property or planet

Earlier we mentioned how re-readings of Marx have contributed to a convergence of red and green ideas. Here we offer our own contribution to such a re-reading. Marx, we suggest, is not only relevant to ecological concerns because of his studies in the early forms of environmental science. His relevance also lies in what he can tell us about a sustainable mode of production that could replace capitalism and its ravaging of the planet. Hints of this are to be found towards the end of *Capital* Volume 3, where Marx makes the following arresting statement:

> From the standpoint of a higher socioeconomic formation, the private property of particular individuals in the earth will appear just as absurd as the private property of one man in other men. Even an entire society, a nation, or all simultaneously existing societies taken together, are not the owners of the earth. They are simply its possessors, its beneficiaries, and have to bequeath it in an improved state to succeeding generations, as *boni patres familias*. (1981: 911, italics in original)

What does Marx mean here? First, we should clarify the terms he uses. The term 'ownership' (*Eigentum*) means a legal relationship of domination (deriving from the Roman law concept of *dominium*), whereas possession (*Besitz*) means a merely factual relation of control: I *have* something at any one moment but I may *lose* it; I have no legal *right* to it. Whereas ownership (*Eigentum*) has 'right' on its side, possession (*Besitz*) is contingent and alterable. Marx, in other words, denies that there is any legitimate basis to property in natural things, let alone the Earth. Second, Marx's striking statement is best understood as a move in the history of ideas: it takes leave of the assumptions which the modern natural law tradition – specifically John Locke – had about the right to appropriate nature. Marx would certainly have known Locke's argument about the legitimate use of nature in his *Two Treatises of Government* (1689). That work contains a defence of private property which left-wing writers uniformly deplore. While we ourselves number among Locke's left-wing critics, we pause to note a complexity in what Locke says. Locke's chapter on 'property' (1986: 129–41) imagines an individual in a state of nature: this individual labours upon nature – and the property thereby carved out becomes theirs.[10] This said, Locke allows (in an eclectic fashion) less 'negative' and more community-based conceptions of property to colour what he says. (A reader of the *Two Treatises* finds a lengthy engagement with the idea that the Earth was given to all in common, an engagement that only makes sense if the assumption was widespread and Locke himself took it seriously.) Locke seems to have made a compromise with widely held commons-based thinking when he stipulated conditions that must be present if the appropriation of nature is to count as 'property' in the full sense. One such condition is that the stock of appropriated things must not be allowed to waste. Another, which concerns us here, is that, when an act of appropriation is carried out, it may be done so only on condition that 'enough, and as good, [is] left in common for others' (Locke 1986: 130).

Marx's statement from *Capital* Volume 3 is subtly but decisively different. There can be no compromise, Marx tells us, between notions of Earth-as-commons and notions of Earth-as-property. Whereas Locke sets out a rationale for a duty towards nature that rests on the rationality of appropriation, Marx does the opposite: property in the Earth is an 'absurd' (*abgesmchackt* – also 'vulgar', 'insipid') idea. The very absurdity of a property in nature is for Marx the rationale for caring for the natural world. Moreover, Marx attaches stronger conditions to this care than does Locke: we are not bidden merely to leave 'enough and as good as' but to 'bequeath it in an *improved* state'. Clearly, this 'improvement' (*Verbesserung*) is not the ideological term used to legitimize the enclosures in capitalism's early phase but a kind of forethought to sustainability and to development. Crucially, it is oriented by principles other than appropriation, labour and value.

Care for the natural world and for future human generations, Marx's words show, requires abandoning notions of property altogether. But what should replace property and what should replace capitalism as the mode of production in which we 'metabolize' sustainably with nature? If we keep in view what we know of Marx's critique of property (both private and state-owned) and his commitment to mutual recognition, we suggest the following conclusion is inescapable: only the practice of *commoning* meets the requirements Marx sets out. Only if the Earth is treated as a commons and production is oriented alike to both human and non-human needs can we be faithful to Marx's demand to bequeath the planet in a better state to future generations.

Let us explain. Commoning has unique qualities, not only in economic terms but also as a form of human interaction. It is a form of production that is uniquely placed to cultivate social relations of freedom and equality. Commoning is, so to say, *the mode of production of mutual recognition*. It is a form of interaction that is cooperative, but more than this, it involves recognizing the needs of the other that allows the other to determine his or her own life. It involves, moreover, *responsibility* and *foresight*. Only through a conversation about what each individual needs and how these needs are to be met on a continuing basis is a sustainable use of resources possible. This conversation is necessarily ongoing; it is taken up again and again wherever resources are to be used. If we were to criticize existing theories of the commons, it is by saying that they lack a full-fledged politics: a theory of the mutual recognition that is necessary for a commons to be sustained. Commoning must, we argue, be fully participatory. It must be 'horizontal' in the sense we have used the term throughout. No state may decide what goods are commoned if freedom is to be maintained. Conversely, individualism is ruled out by the very cooperative (i.e. recognitive) character of commoning. If a 'tragic' use of the commons occurs, it is precisely where this conversation fails to occur or is broken-off and self-interest takes over: individuals return to sphere-based self-conceptions of freedom and 'rights' and fail to recognize the other.

Commoning, we suggest, rather than being a relic of pre-capitalist life, is the 'higher socio-economic formation' Marx alludes to in the afore-cited quotation from *Capital*. It is from the 'higher' vantage point of a commoning relationship that property in the natural world looks 'absurd'. Commoning, we propose, is what Marx means when he writes of 'a conscious and rational treatment of the land as . . . the inalienable condition for the existence and reproduction of the chain of human generations' (1981: 949). Put another way, a *common sense about the commons* (to adapt E. P. Thompson's phrase) must be present for production and consumption to be sustainable on a long-term basis. Yet 'common sense' is not simply a precondition of commoning, because commoning generates its own common sense: we cultivate mutual recognition whenever we cultivate the earth together; the two practices form a virtual circle. The idea of a *common sense of the commons* translates Marx's demand to bequeath the planet in a better state and strips the rationale of environmentalism from any taint of Lockean possessive individualism.[11]

Engels once wrote that 'we by no means rule (*beherrschen*) over nature like a conqueror over a foreign people, like someone standing outside nature . . . [but] we, with flesh, blood and brain, belong to nature, and exist in its midst' (Marx and Engels 1987a: 461). Marx, as we have seen, shares this insight when he theorizes an exchange or 'metabolism' between humans and the environment, a metabolism that is both complex and fragile (1981: 949–50; cf. Schmidt 1971: 89–90). What Marx's scattered reflections on nature suggests to us is that humans prove dependent upon their environment in the very moment they seem independent of it, that the exchange between the two is a fine balance, and that any subjugation of nature would be contradictory and unsustainable. It is as if Marx carries over the insights of the dialectic of master and slave into his thinking about the natural world.

The capitalist organization of production is a unique threat to the ecological fabric which makes human life possible. It makes of humans a force of nature unprecedented in historical terms.[12] To quote Engels once more, 'man alone has succeeded in impressing his stamp on nature, not only by shifting plant and animal species from one place to another, but also by so altering the aspect and climate of his dwelling-place, and even the plants and animals themselves, that the consequences of his activity can disappear only with the general extinction of the terrestrial globe' (Marx and Engels 1987a: 330). The task facing us – daunting though it is – is to put our elemental power to use and to stop capitalism, to make of our planet a place fit to live in, a place, that is, of mutual recognition.

A view of *commoning as the mode of production of mutual recognition* is, for us, the starting point of this task. Commoning, as we saw in Chapter 4, is not necessarily just a local undertaking but can be 'scaled up' to address national and international issues concerning natural resources. In doing so, there is no need to sacrifice the 'horizontal' decision-making which mutual recognition entails. No despotic Climate Leviathan is the logical outcome of a climate crisis that is global in scale.

Rather, the cooperation that will be needed to solve the crisis can be a collective exercise in self-determination. To quote from the Belém Declaration of global ecological activists, 'collective policy-making on the local, regional, national, and international levels amounts to society's exercise of communal freedom and responsibility' (The Belém Declaration, cited in Löwy 2015: 89).[13]

The idea of commoning as the mode of production of mutual recognition is, we suggest, the consistent implication of Marx's writings. Given this, it is unsurprising that in another of his late works, the 'Ethnological Notebooks' (contemporary with the 'Ecological Notebooks' discussed previously), Marx began to make fascinating links between democracy, freedom and natural sustainability. Marx's little-discussed but intriguing late studies of the anthropology of propertyless societies – particularly the Iroquois people – view these not as 'relics' of a 'primitive communism' (he dispenses with any 'stagist' or 'unilineal' theory of historical development) but as models for possible ways forward. As Raya Dunayevska notes, the late Marx turned to anthropology 'not for purposes of discovering new origins, but for perceiving new revolutionary forces' (Dunayevskaya 1981: 187; for discussion see Rosemont 1989). A reading of the 'Ethnological Notebooks' (which space forbids undertaking here) would show that in the indigenous societies he studied, Marx found a property-free subsistence coinciding with direct democracy and an ecological sensibility. It is, for example, not just the Iroquois' lack of property that seems to fascinate Marx but their 'democratic assembly where every adult male and female member had a voice upon all questions brought before it' (Marx 1974: 150) along with their veneration of 'the Earth for the various productions which had ministered to [their] sustenance' (Marx 1974: 169).[14]

All of which suggests that it is hasty to view the practices of commoning and direct democracy – instances of mutual recognition we have discussed – as utopian or idealistic. On the contrary, such practices have long been the 'common sense' of many peoples across the globe; today, they are still widespread in regions that have not been wholly integrated into the capitalist system.[15] These are not to be dismissed as 'archaic' relics but should be seen as sites and models of resistance. Engels's infamous critique of 'utopian socialism' has blinded us to the resources that living examples of alternative social existence offer to the revolutionary Left. It is no coincidence that in worlds without property the 'sense of having', so typical of capitalist society (Marx and Engels 1975a: 300), is absent and – to quote Marx's favourite anthropologist, Lewis Henry Morgan – a 'law of hospitality' operates which '[t]ends to the equalization of subsistence' (cited in Linebaugh 2019: 59). It is no coincidence that in such worlds conviviality rather than domination is the typical attitude towards nature.[16] To see this is in turn to see something of the monstrous reality of capitalist development. The 'primitive accumulation' of which Marx wrote – the severing of peoples from their means of subsistence and their shackling to wage labour – is a history not only of genocide but also of the annihilation of countless relationships of ecological symbiosis. When Marx says that this history is 'written in letters of blood and fire' (1976: 875; cf. Caffentzis 2013: 6–7) the dreadful ecological cost is to be witnessed too.

Recognition's environment

Our book has presented mutual recognition – by which we mean recognition in its Left-Hegelian sense – as the rationale of anti-capitalist struggle. The emancipation towards which anti-capitalist struggle aims is a freedom where mutual recognition obtains. If anti-capitalist struggle is broadened to include struggle on ecological issues, does it mean that such struggle has two rationales (red and green), one of which must take priority? Our answer is no. The two rationales are two aspects of the same goal. Readers of our book will recollect days when humanity's impact on nature was seen as a question that might be addressed once capitalism had been overturned. Here, we take it that such days are over. Humanity's impact on nature is to be addressed in and through anti-capitalist struggle itself. This is a key principle behind the activism of much of the climate justice movement today, along with countless indigenous struggles which acknowledge the disproportionate impact of climate change on those who have done so little to cause it.

Yet how exactly can recognition do justice to the green rationale of preserving a sustainable and flourishing environment? One way of answering this is metaphorical. If one recognizes other people as self-determining, one avoids destroying or impoverishing the environment in which those individuals exist. In recognizing an other, one attempts to maintain the complexity and the many-sidedness of his or her world. One maintains the interest – the social and natural and moral and aesthetic interest – of his or her world. If this interest is diminished or, for example, reduced to a single imperative (say, the imperative of survival), his or her space for self-determination is contradicted. Contradictory recognition prevails. When one visits a habitation of people whom one regards as friends, trashing the habitation's contents trashes the friendship itself.

Let us take this point to its logical conclusion. Let us imagine, in a dystopian fashion, a scenario in which the world's flora have burned away to desert and its fauna have been decimated by mass extinction. Let us imagine furthermore a world in which the inhabitable land mass has been greatly reduced by rising seas, seas which in turn have turned acidic and lifeless. And let us ask, in such a world, what forms of human recognition may exist? Only one form of self-determination seems conceivable. Only one form of self-determination makes sense: Is survival possible? If recognition is, as we have argued, absolutely integral to what an individual is, then to strip an individual down to a single possibility – to strip life down from the conditions of its true flourishing to that of its mere survival – condemns individuals to a drastically impoverished degree of freedom. Survival in this notional world may or may not be possible. But it hardly matters whether it is. The destruction of a diverse and thriving environment is already the onset of death.

This point can be made in yet another way. The potential trajectory of climate change mentioned in the previous paragraph underlines the destruction of the imagination that would be our lot in such a dystopia. Aesthetic life perishes once ecological dystopia is achieved. If humans exist in a social way through recognition, they require habitats where variety thrives.[17] They require not just mutual recognition but a natural 'background' which gives life and meaning to that recognition and which can sustain it. 'Life', Hegel says in the *Phenomenology*, is 'the natural setting' of recognition (1977: 114).

The natural world – vibrant and diverse or blighted and desolate – is the integral background to every act of recognition. Once we realize this, the recognitive circle is widened and enriched – its depth is brought into relief. When Silvia Federici – in a quote we already cited in Chapter 4 – suggests redefining the word 'community' as 'a quality of relations, a principle of cooperation, and of responsibility to each other and to the earth, the forests, the seas, the animals' (Federici 2019: 110) she seems to have mutually recognitive relations in mind. But what about 'the animals', with whom the passage concludes? Does Federici mean to suggest that, between animals and humans, mutual recognition exists? There is, we suggest, no need to read her in this fashion. Common experience shows that it is difficult to be certain how much reciprocity is present in a specific human/animal interaction and that the danger of anthropomorphism is real. Yet there is sometimes more reciprocity than a human wishes to admit. The passage from Federici does not stipulate a theory of animals and humans. It wishes us to view the natural environment in an inclusive and open-ended sense. For our part, we suggest that if we regard human beings in a mutually recognitive fashion, as Federici implies, we already have the theoretical justification for caring for the other's (i.e. our shared) environment.

What recognition recognizes is not only human self-determination but the social and a natural setting to our self-determination. It recognizes that each human has a 'world', in the phenomenological sense of the term. Part of what mutual recognition accentuates, and throws into relief, is the set of preconditions – the practical and natural preconditions – that must be fulfilled if action is to have a self-determining cast. If social oppression obtains, and if recognition is contradictory, the self-determination of individuals exists in an alienated way. If ecological conditions are disregarded by a society ruled by 'market logic' (Klein) and if our 'world' becomes drastically degraded, then self-determination is constrained and distorted.[18] In a wasteland, the projects that are open to an individual are reduced to one. He or she seeks not to thrive but to survive.

If these points are allowed, environmentalist concern ceases to be a plank or issue that may be laid, separately, alongside recognition-based goals. There can be no question of a trade-off between ecological and recognition-based theory. On the contrary, a politics of mutual recognition includes and encompasses environmentalist concerns. A consistent politics of mutual recognition is a fight for a vibrant, diverse and abundant nature that can also allow humans, *qua* recognitive beings, to flourish. It can only be a red–green politics. Red and green demands – when viewed in the light of recognition – flow together.

Whether the foregoing remarks satisfy the 'deep ecologist' whom we imagined here is difficult to say. Whether they satisfy the orthodox Marxist with his or her Promethean dreams is likewise uncertain. If they do not, then he or she parts company with Gunn and Wilding's red–green approach. What we have shown is that environmentalist and recognition-based issues need not merely be laid alongside each other. Environmental concern is inescapable if a politics of mutual recognition is pressed to its end. To profess indifference to recognition's environment is to contradict oneself.

Climate change cannot but be a central concern of the Left. It is central because it threatens the very possibility of the mutual recognition which – our book has argued – is the goal and life of anti-capitalist struggle. Our aim in this chapter was not just to discuss climate change through the lens of recognition but to demonstrate how political issues can be addressed in a recognitive – and thus revolutionary – way. The number of issues which are recognitively relevant could, we believe, be extended much further. That, however, would be the subject of another book. It suffices here to say that the notion of recognition serves, when understood in what we have termed a *Phenomenology*-style fashion, to draw together issues that are crucial to present-day radical thought. Our discussion vindicates the core argument of the book: that mutual recognition is a conception that the radical Left may endorse, to clarify its thinking – and needs.

Conclusion

'Recognition', we have shown, is the term that unlocks neoliberal mystification and provides a new foundation for revolutionary anti-capitalism. But it does so only on condition that it is understood aright. The notion of recognition articulates present-day revolution if and only if it is viewed in what, for us, is a Hegelian and Marxian sense. In Chapters 1 and 2 we explained what, in our view, these terms entail. By a 'Hegelian' view of recognition, we understand the view taken in Hegel's *Phenomenology of Spirit* – as distinct from the view taken in his later *Philosophy of Right*. Our argument is that the *Phenomenology* is by far the most incisive and politically challenging of Hegel's works. The *Phenomenology*'s message, we maintain, is that recognition is the essence of social existence. Yet only a recognition which is non-contradictory – for Hegel one that *eschews domination and rejects institutions* – is recognition in its full and proper and mutual sense. By a 'Marxian' (or authentically 'Marxist') view, we understand the position which Marx adopts in the 1840s, for example, in his *Comments on James Mill* and his *1844 Manuscripts*, and which he later develops in the *Grundrisse* and *Capital*. Marx's position, we argued, takes up the revolutionary notion of recognition found in Hegel's *Phenomenology*. Stated differently, Hegel's *Phenomenology* and Marx's writings rest on one and the same recognition-based view. Marx's understanding of communism is in effect a reworking of Hegelian mutual recognition. When viewed against this (Left-) Hegelian background and when the continuity (rather than the difference) between Hegel and Marx is emphasized, key Marxian concepts (exchange, property, class and communism) appear in their true revolutionary light.

In Chapter 3 we assessed and rejected a set of approaches that have come to dominate debates on recognition – approaches advocated by Charles Taylor, Axel Honneth and their followers. Taylor, so we argued, draws recognition onto liberal terrain, failing to see the alienations involved in a world divided into cultural groupings and identities, no matter how equally esteemed these groupings or identities are. Honneth attempts to link recognition to critical theory but betrays that tradition by taking his cue from the institutions of the capitalist world – in essence the same 'spheres' of family, civil society and state pictured in Hegel's late *Philosophy of Right*. Even when, on Honneth's model, these 'spheres' are taken to have an internal dynamic that tends towards greater freedom, the horizons of Honneth's world view remain as circumscribed as those of the late Hegel. Contra Honneth, the institutions of the present world are by no means the ultimate horizon of politics, and a social democratic reformism offers little hope to the Left.

Our book has made the case for a *revolutionary recognition* – mutual recognition as a revolutionary not a liberal or reformist category. Our discussion was not just a debate in the history of ideas, however, but sought at every turn to underline its political topicality. The mutual recognition championed by Hegel in his *Phenomenology* and by Marx throughout his life is crucial to an understanding of present-day politics. It is the theoretical fundament on which a consistent radical politics – a grassroots and horizontalist politics – can rest. In a word, Hegel's *Phenomenology* may be read not merely as a philosophical classic but as a revolutionary resource. As set out in Chapter 4, recent waves of struggle – above all the global uprising of social movements since 2011 – point to recognition as a living idea. The struggles that began in those years can be regarded as prefigurative experiments in forms that mutual recognition may take. In placing both hierarchies and institutions radically in question, today's anti-capitalism is heir to both Hegel's and Marx's thought.

Since Hegel's and Marx's time the 'dangerous idea' of mutual recognition has been kept alive by a range of thinkers who we have quoted in the pages of this book. One such thinker is Ernst Bloch, for whom 'a society without masters and slaves is clearly the very thing sought for so long – and in vain – under the name of humanization. It is the very thing that a class society has so long opposed or impeded – together with the substance of hope, which is only in the process of formation' (Bloch 1971: 27).

Such a formulation can mislead, however, if it presents only an auspicious history, a *vita nova* and not also an *inferno*. This is never more relevant than today, in the face of a perilous climate emergency (discussed in Chapter 5) and a resurgent Right intent on enacting a brutal disaster capitalism. Against this dark background no communist politics can with any honesty be sanguine. There is no arc of history that bends inevitably towards justice. Barbarism, whether social or ecological, is just as possible an outcome. The hope of a politics of mutual recognition is – to this extent – counterfactual, a hope against hope, against the most powerful tendencies of capitalist society.

Revolutionary Recognition offers no easy consolation to the reader. Not least because the mutual recognition it champions would do away with those very institutions and social roles which, even in the most alienated of capitalist societies, offer some *security* – a beguiling and bewitching security – in both an emotional and political sense. A mutually recognitive freedom is *more exposed* than was the case where alienation prevails. Being uncontradicted, self-determination stands out in starker relief – and is all the more vulnerable for that. The cost of ending alienation is that the quasi-natural security it offers becomes an untenable dream.

At the end of the line of argument that our book has followed, questions inevitably remain. The questions, we suggest, likely divide into two sorts. How may a transition from contradicted to uncontradicted recognition be envisaged? How may mutual recognition's interactive process be sustained? In closing, we comment briefly on these two questions.

How might a transition from contradictory to mutual recognition be envisaged? In an archived interview, Max Horkheimer expresses views which seem to tell against our claims. 'Critical theory', he states there, 'is based on the idea that one cannot determine what is good'; we cannot determine this because 'we lack the means' (Horkheimer 1969). Critical theory belongs, in other words, in a world where alienation is so deep that emancipation cannot be pictured. How, in such a world, is critique possible? Horkheimer indicates a possibility: 'we can bring up the negative aspect of this [the alienated] society' (Horkheimer 1969). Horkheimer's words seem to contradict our own because, for him, emancipation is hidden – whereas for us the mutually recognitive character of emancipation is plain. Between Horkheimer's words and our own there is, let us agree, a difference of emphasis. But is there an incompatibility? We doubt that there is. At the same time, we concede that the issue of transition is shrouded in obscurity. A movement from contradicted to uncontradicted recognition cannot, realistically, be pictured as a straightforward and unambiguous leap from what is dark to what is light. Just as hierarchical patterns persist into a post-revolutionary society, so mutual recognition may arise already in a pre-revolutionary society – in a fragmentary and prefigurative way. In a transitional epoch, it is impossible to decide what *can* and *cannot* be clearly seen. To these difficulties, a further complication may be added: a world where recognition is contradicted is, in Hegel's expression, an inverted world. In a world which is inverted, glimpses forward are possible and, at the same time, denied. Nothing is what it seems. Horkheimer's seeming pessimism ('we lack the means') and our own invocation of mutual recognition strike us as intertwining voices in a region where everything is shifting and uncertainty prevails.

How may mutual recognition be sustained? First, let us focus on mutual recognition as a process. The process is unbounded in every sense: the individuality that it allows to come into its own is not constrained by the acting out of a role definition (or role definitions), hierarchy and prejudice are cast aside, human interaction is limitless since mutual recognition is extended to all others, and the 'conversation' in which mutual recognition consists addresses all relevant topics. Such a view of recognition dovetails, we have suggested, with a view of revolution which does more than replace one set of social frameworks (or social institutions and roles) with another. It dovetails with revolution which calls political organization into question and with revolutionary action which affirms self-determination.

All this said, mutual recognition is not a utopia: possibilities of bad faith continue (as we have seen, with reference to Hegel) and relations of good faith have to be continually remade. Mutual recognition knows no natural or quasi-natural inertia: although it is humane, there is no question of humanity's realizing its 'true essence' – or 'true nature'. Lacking quasi-natural security, mutual recognition lacks the stability that inertia brings. At each stage in the existence of such a form of life, a relapse into *what Hegel terms* 'history' and *what Marx terms* 'hitherto existing society' remains a possibility. No guarantees against a relapse are conceivable. More than this, what may be termed ontological insecurity and mutual recognition are inseparable. In the margins of a text describing mutual recognition, hints of existential horror appear. We quote Ernst Bloch once more:

> The course of liberation . . . is . . . not aimed at facilitating somnolence or generalising the pleasurable, comfortable leisure of the contemporary upper classes. We do not propose to end up with the world of Dickens, or to warm ourselves at the fireplaces of Victorian England, at best. The goal, the eminently practical goal, and the basic motive of socialist ideology is this: to give to every man not just a job but his own distress, wretchedness, misery and darkness, his own buried, summoning light; to give to everyone's life a Dostoevskyan touch. (1970: 60)

How may emancipation be sustained? No *definitive* answer to this question may be given. A *provisional* answer, and an answer that must be renewed at each point when threats emerge, can only be found in the process – the interactive process – of mutual recognition itself. We must learn to identify tensile strengths which mutual recognition contains. We must, for example, learn to think of *good faith* not in a moralistic way that is attached to altruism but as a form of recognitive practice. We must guard against lapses into history (or into alienation) not by erecting legal safeguards but by being vigilant for changes in recognition – for example, a change from an egalitarian (or horizontal) to an institutional (or hierarchical) form. We must confront insecurity not by building possessive individualist enclaves but by developing perspectives which *freedom through others* brings.

Our book has sought to bring back to life Hegel's revolutionary notion of recognition and to present it as both the goal and the core of anti-capitalist struggle. We have breathed fresh life into a position that, in the neoliberal period, has been neglected or reduced to an eviscerated shell. Such a description of our book is accurate – but incomplete.

Besides attempting to renew a school of thought, however vital, we have presented our discussion in political terms. The Left-Hegelian line of thought which we have renewed is, we believe, essential to struggle today. A politics based on *Phenomenology*-style recognition meets the challenge of today's revolutionary movements. If the book has been found convincing, 'mutual recognition' will become the watchword of anti-capitalist struggle. The lexicon of revolution will be written anew, and glimmers of a self-determining future will appear through the neoliberal fog.

NOTES

Foreword

1 See, for example, the critiques by Edith González, 'The Construction of a Conceptual Prison', and Panagiotis Doulos, 'Common Paradoxes', both in Barbagallo, Beuret and Harvie (2019).

Introduction

1 On this concept, see Luxemburg (2004: 250). We discuss 'the problem of organization' in Chapter 4.

2 A revolutionary organization sees itself as 'prefigurative' when it attempts to anticipate and embody the social change at which it aims. See Chapter 4.

3 For an influential use of the term 'prefiguration', see Rowbotham, Segal and Wainwright (1979).

4 See, for example, David Graeber's *The Democracy Project* (2013) – still, we consider, the best book-length treatment of Occupy's themes.

5 On horizontalism, see Graeber (2013) once again.

6 For a passage where Marx is directly critical of social democracy, see Marx and Engels (1978: 283): 'Alongside . . . new official [social democratic] governments they [the victorious workers] must establish their own revolutionary governments, whether in the form of workers' clubs or workers' committees so that the bourgeois-democratic governments not only immediately lose the support of the workers but from the outset see themselves supervised and threatened by authorities backed by the whole mass of the workers. In a word, from the first moment of victory, mistrust must be directed not only by the defeated reactionary party, but against the workers' previous allies, against the party that wishes to

exploit the common victory for itself alone.' The passage is quoted by Vasilis Grollios in his *Negativity and Democracy* (Grollios 2017: 54).

7 The phrase 'scarcely imagined' is, of course, an exaggeration: in the twentieth century, radical thought encompassed a galaxy of utopian and 'Left Apocalyptic' themes. Besides social democratic politicians, the Left was made of anarchists and artists and psychoanalysts and critical theorists – and experimenters in a new life. The themes that were, thus, brought into focus become *scarcely imaginable* only if seen in social democratic terms.

Chapter 1

1 Our discussion refers to Miller's translation of the *Phenomenology* (Hegel 1977). A reader of German is pointed towards the original (Hegel 1970).

2 In *Being and Nothingness*, Sartre writes of 'the famous "Master-Slave" relation which so profoundly influenced Marx. We need not enter here into its details. It is sufficient to observe that the Slave is the Truth of the Master. But this unilateral recognition is unequal and insufficient, for the truth of his self-certitude for the Master is a non-essential consciousness' (Sartre 2003: 261).

3 Here we differ strongly with Kojève, who reads too much into Hegel's cryptic suggestion (1977: 118–19) that the slave puts himself to work (*Arbeit*) in the cause of liberation, making of the master-slave passage an almost Stakhanovite homage to labour (see 1969: 22–8). Hegel clearly cannot mean to say that slave labour is liberating. Instead what he is pointing to is a formative, self-educative activity that informs freedom. The slave is, in effect, learning to revolt.

4 Susan Buck-Morss (2009) argues persuasively that the key inspiration for Hegel was not only the French Revolution but also the Haitian Revolution of 1791–804, an uprising which, under the banner 'Liberty or Death!', overthrew colonial slavery on the Caribbean island and placed the wider Atlantic slave system in question. Hegel was indeed an avid reader of news of the Haiti events, as documents prove, and it is highly likely that his thoughts on the relation of master and slave were inspired by those of racial exploitation. Hegel, we argue, targets *all* forms of domination; this is what makes his idea of mutual recognition so revolutionary, so 'dangerous'.

5   In the Preface to the *Phenomenology*, Hegel claims that absolute (free) being 'is essentially a *result*' (1977: 11, emphasis in original). This claim makes sense only if *freedom* and *self-determination* are equated.

6   Whether Hegel thought in terms of an 'end of history' remains controversial among commentators. His remark, in the *Phenomenology*'s final chapter, that 'until spirit ... has completed itself as world-spirit, it cannot reach its consummation as self-conscious spirit' (1977: 488) suggests that, in that work at least, he thought in such terms.

7   Rousseau is clearly a touchstone for Hegel's argument, but does he also draw on the earlier idea of La Boétie (1530–63) that political power rests solely on the consent of the subjugated? La Boétie certainly saw the element of dependence and fragility in domination. For further discussion, see Gunn and Wilding (2012).

8   For historical detail, see Rude (1959), especially p. 9. Jean-Paul Sartre's notion of a 'group-in-fusion' (see 2004) takes up the dynamic that such crowd activity involves. In a group-in-fusion, we may note, there is no division of labour between a *leader* and *the lead*. It is true that, in the insurrectionary crowd that stormed the Bastille, someone – some individual – must have cried 'To the Bastille!' first. But the individual who thus cried was not a leader and the crowd which stormed the Bastille did not act on instructions. *Anyone* – anyone in the crowd – might have spoken the words that were on the crowd's lips.

9   Adorno rightly notes that 'the splitting of the Hegelian school into a left and right wing was founded in the ambiguity of the theory no less than in the political situation preceding the 1848 revolution' (1978: 244–5).

10 See Williams (1997: Part Two), Pippin (2000: 155, 164–7), Fraser and Honneth (2003: 143–6), Honneth (2010: 50), Honneth (2012: Ch. 2), Anderson (2009: Ch. 6).

11 The word 'rightful' calls for explanation. For the *Philosophy of Right*, a social order is (we consider) rightful when all important virtues and all important knowledge are inscribed within it. Such a society may – according to the Hegel of the *Philosophy of Right* – nevertheless be one which is class-divided and premised on a social division of labour. Our worry is that an individual member of such a society will have access to only *some* of the virtues (and *part* of the knowledge) that is possessed by society overall. Our worry is that such an individual lives out a life where institution-based recognition predominates – and where, in a word, alienation prevails.

12 Hegel describes property as 'the *existence* [*Dasein*] of personality' – and then goes on to add that the '*existence* which my willing thereby attains' includes 'its ability to be recognized [*Erkennbarkeit*] by others' (2008: 65). Why *Erkennbarkeit* rather than *Anerkennbarkeit*? If the term were *Anerkennbarkeit*, Hegel's claim might be that property has a practical, normative force only when it is recognized. Since the term used is *Erkennbarkeit*, Hegel (the Hegel of the *Philosophy of Right*) seems to imply that, on the contrary, property's existence is a social fact to be acknowledged and respected. The quoted passage strikes us as relinquishing the great insights of the *Phenomenology*.

13 Adorno writes, 'As though the dialectic had become frightened of itself, in the *Philosophy of Right* Hegel broke off his thoughts by abruptly absolutizing one category – the state' (1993: 80). We add just one qualification: what Adorno (along with many other readers of Hegel) calls 'the dialectic' must be understood as the movement of contradictory recognition.

14 In the Preface to the *Philosophy of Right* Hegel famously declares that 'what is rational is actual and what is actual is rational' (2008: 14). We are aware, however, that the published version of the *Philosophy of Right* differs from the lecture notes upon which Hegel's book was based. In the lectures notes (taken by his students), Hegel states things differently: 'what is rational will become actual, and what is actual will become rational' (1983: 51), that is, a rationally free polity is yet to be realized. This would certainly change the tenor of the *Philosophy of Right*, but it does not undermine our point: Hegel's polity, whether realized or not, is conformist in ways that his early work is not.

15 Lukács writes of Hegel's gradual '"reconciliation" with the existing state of affairs in Germany' (1975: 453). Whereas the Preface to the *Phenomenology* spoke of a revolutionary 'dawn', the Preface to the *Philosophy of Right* speaks of 'the falling of dusk' (1975: 456).

16 Hans-Georg Flickinger is one of the few recent authors to highlight the political significance of the difference between the two works. He writes, 'If we agree that the *Phenomenology of Spirit* carries through the stages of social recognition up to their highest form . . . then we can use Hegel's argumentation as a critical foil against the idea of an ethical life reduced to its liberal, merely legal form [in the *Philosophy of Right*]' (Flickinger 2008: 107).

17 The Lacanian idea of an inevitable and insuperable misrecognition (*méconnaissance*) between humans shares nothing with Hegel's approach. That this pessimistic view of recognition has nevertheless been influential can

be seen from the popularity of Slavoj Žižek's writings during the early years of the twenty-first century. For discussion see Thomas Bedorf's *Verkennende Anerkennung* (2010).

18 In her work of 1949, *The Second Sex*, Simone de Beauvoir says that 'certain passages in the argument employed by Hegel in defining the relation of master to slave apply much better to the relation of man to woman' (de Beauvoir 1956: 90). Frantz Fanon, in his 1952 work *Black Skin, White Masks*, notes that 'the only way to break the vicious circle [of oppression] is to restore to the other his human reality, different from his natural reality, by way of mediation and recognition. The other, however, must perform a similar operation. "Action from one side only would be useless, because what is to happen can only be brought about by means of both. . . . They recognize themselves as mutually recognizing each other"' (Fanon 2007: 192, citing Hegel). The radicality of this post-war reception of Hegel, its *ceterum censeo* of domination, has today sadly been forgotten.

Chapter 2

1 When Maurizio Lazzarato, in his analysis of the *Comments on James Mill*, refers to the element of 'self-constitution' and 'subjectivation' in the creditor–debtor relation, he unwittingly refers to the constitutive power of recognition (here, contradictory recognition) upon subjectivity. See Lazzarato (2011: 55 and 59). The theme of recognition goes unmentioned in Lazzarato's otherwise useful book.

2 What in Marx's early work appears as moral inversion appears in the late work as a *Lichtbild*. Marx's metaphor comes from early photography: just as a photographic slide inverts reality, so capitalism presents to us a world through the looking glass (Marx 1973: 249). On Marx (like Hegel) as theorist of the *verkehrte Welt*, see H. Reichelt (2005).

3 It is not surprising that capital's 'domination' (*Herrschaft*) over labour is a common motif in *Capital* (see, for example, Marx 1975: 386, 390, 526, 645, 648, 765) and though on occasion Marx contrasts it with 'immediate relations of domination and servitude (*unmittelbaren Herrschafts- und Knechtschaftsverhältnissen*)' (Marx 1975: 93, 354), it is clear he means by this that capitalist domination (in contrast to other modes of production) is highly

mediated, highly 'impersonal' (to use William Clare Roberts's expression – 2017: 82). Domination under capitalism it is exerted not so much by a particular Lord (as in feudalism or slavery) as by the Lordship of capital as such.

4 Marx continues, 'In all previous revolutions the mode of activity always remained un-changed and it was only a question of a different distribution of this activity, a new distribution of labour to other persons, whilst the communist revolution is directed against the hitherto existing mode of activity, does away with labour and abolishes the rule of all classes with the classes themselves' (Marx and Engels 1976a: 52).

5 On Marx as critic of labour, see Holloway (2010: 87–99), Cleaver (2000: 127–31) and Postone (1993: 123–85).

6 Marx notes drily that he by no means depicts the capitalist 'in rosy colours' (1976: 92). But it seems to us he could have added the same about the worker, since both roles involve misrecognition. Of course one role is more 'comfortably' misrecognized, comfortably alienated than the other.

7 A point we believe to be consistent with the claim of the *1844 Manuscripts* (Marx and Engels 1975a: 270) that 'we have proceeded from the premises of political economy. We have accepted its language and laws. . . . On the basis of political economy itself, in its own words, we have shown that the worker sinks to the level of a commodity, and becomes indeed the most wretched of commodities.'

8 In the *1844 Manuscripts*, Marx notes that *even when capitalist economies are booming and wages rising*, the worker 'declines[s] to a mere machine, a bond servant (*Knecht*) of capital' (Marx and Engels 1975a: 238).

9 The critique of 'having' (as opposed to 'being') will be familiar to readers of Erich Fromm. But it seems Fromm was largely unaware of their origin in Marx. In answer to Fromm's letter asking her where to look in Marx for this concept, Dunayevskaya replies 'the concept of To Be/To Have is so pivotal to [Marx's] life's work from the moment he broke with bourgeois society in 1843 until the day of his death in 1883 that it is a challenge to pin down' (Dunayevskaya 2012: 174).

10 If a reader adopts the standpoint of the protagonist in Knut Hamsun's *Hunger* (2016), a good many of the interconnections in *Capital* become clear.

11 In Raymond Chandler's *The High Window*, Philip Marlowe enters a region beyond Bay City where 'the road was lined with walled and fenced estates. Some had high walls, some had low walls, some had ornamental iron fences, some

were a bit old-fashioned and got along with tall hedges' (1951: 34). Marlowe is entering an upmarket version of the society that, for Marx, capitalism brings.

12 In his *The Political Theory of Possessive Individualism*, C. B. Macpherson links possessive individualism to the notion that the individual is 'essentially the proprietor of his own person or capacities' (1962: 3). That is, he links possessive individualism to the notion of self-ownership. We, for our part, prefer a broader definition: we think of possessive individualism as being present wherever the individual is pictured in property-based terms.

13 See, especially, Rousseau 1984: 118–19. In the *Discourse on Inequality*, Rousseau writes as a fierce critic of the modern natural law tradition – which was, in the days before political economy, property-based thinking's chief cultural 'carrier'.

14 In his *Rupturing the Dialectic*, Harry Cleaver draws attention to this difference or distinction (see 2017: 110, n. 5). We are grateful to Cleaver for his perceptive reading.

15 Cf. Dunayevskaya (1981: 182–3), where she notes that Marx condemns both 'private' and 'collective' property.

16 Around the base-and-superstructure image, a Marxist orthodoxy has arisen. Here, we do not discuss the image – save to note an incoherence that it contains: in picturing an economic base, so to say 'superstructural' elements are already present. Regarding the orthodoxy, we offer an observation: despite its incoherence, the model of base and superstructure is still widely (if tacitly) employed. All too frequently, an understanding of Marx relies sotto voce on a diluted version of the base-and-superstructure model.

17 In Althusser's memorable words, 'the reader will know how Volume Three [of *Capital*] ends: A title: *Classes*. Forty lines, then silence' (Althusser and Balibar 1970: 193). The 'forty lines' are not, however, devoid of significance: it is there that Marx rejects *source of revenue* as a criterion of class.

18 In an anecdote told about Flaubert, something close to a *downward-facing parabola* appears: 'Henry Céard recounts how, one evening in Flaubert's apartment in the Rue Murillo, he told the veteran novelist of the admiration he felt for *Sentimental Education*. Obviously moved by this unexpected tribute, Flaubert drew himself up to his full height and answered in a gruff voice: "So you like it, do you? All the same, the book is doomed to failure, because it doesn't do this." He put his long, powerful hands together in the shape of a pyramid. "The public," he explained, "wants works which exalt its illusions, whereas *Sentimental*

Education..." And here he turned his big hands upside down and opened them as if to let his dreams fall into a bottomless pit...' (Translator's Introduction to Flaubert 1964: 13).

19 One more quotation may help to drive home our interpretation. Marx writes in *Capital*, 'A man... neither enters into the world in possession of a mirror, nor as a Fichtean philosopher who can say "I am I"; man first sees and recognises himself in another man. Peter only relates to himself as a man through his relation to another man, Paul, in whom he recognizes his likeness. With this, however, Paul also becomes from head to toe, in his physical form as Paul, the form of appearance of the species man for Peter' (1976: 144, footnote).

20 Brecht's *Threepenny Opera* closes with the following lines: 'For some are in darkness / And others are in light / And you see the ones in brightness / Those in darkness drop from sight.'

21 Our use of the phrase 'in the last instance' is intended to guard against a misunderstanding. In stressing the centrality of mutual recognition, we do not attempt to downplay (or claim that Marx attempts to downplay) more specific social and political goals. No doubt, it may be asked whether such a goal is a *precondition of* mutual recognition or a part, so to say, a 'moment') of mutual recognition itself. We do not discuss this issue here.

22 Or does it? Marx says that the *free development of each* is the condition for the *free development of all*. Can this proposition be reversed? Can we be sure that, for Marx, the *free development of all* is the condition for the *free development of each*? Given Marx's hostility to monadological or 'atomic' individualism, it seems reasonable to see him as endorsing the following position: the *free development of each* and the *free development of all* presuppose one another.

23 Chitty (1998) rightly argues that a focus on recognition upsets a base-and-superstructure reading. Our suggestion is that, if Marx is understood in terms of recognition, the entire justification for a base-and-superstructure reading disappears.

24 The lengthy literature on Hegelianism in the years after Hegel's death includes Hook (1962) and Toews (1980). Renault (2012) offers a fresh consideration.

25 Such relations are no less ubiquitous today than in Marx's time. As Silvia Federici notes, 'along with impoverishment, unemployment, overwork, homelessness, and debt has gone the increasing criminalisation of the working class, through a mass incarceration policy recalling the seventeenth-century Grand Confinement,

and the formation of an *ex-lege* proletariat made of undocumented immigrant workers, students defaulting loans, producers or sellers of illicit goods, sex workers. It is a multitude of proletarians, existing and labouring in the shadow, reminding us that the production of populations without rights – slaves, indentured servants, peons, convicts, sans papiers – remains a structural necessity of capitalist accumulation' (2008: 105).

Chapter 3

1. By 'procedural' liberalism, Taylor understands the view that 'a liberal society must remain neutral on [the question of what is to count as] the good life, and restrict itself to ensuring that however they see things, citizens deal fairly with one another and the state deals equally with all' (Taylor 1994: 57).

2. While not denying this, we confess ourselves unhappy with the term 'cultural', which strikes us as vague. But we do not pursue this charge of vagueness here.

3. We agree with Taylor that an individual's identity 'crucially depends' on his or her dialogical – indeed, recognitive – 'relations with others' (Taylor 1994: 34). In passing, we note that, our various criticisms of Taylor notwithstanding, we find ourselves in broad agreement with his article's introductory sections.

4. When Taylor himself employs the expression 'politics of difference' (1994: 38), this appears to be the meaning that he has in mind.

5. Honneth (2013: 10): 'we recognize somebody in the expectation that he or she is recognizing us'.

6. Among critics of Honneth, Emmanuel Renault – see especially Renault (2011) – presents arguments that most closely resemble our own position. Renault is, so far as we know, unique in believing (as we do) that spheres of recognition *qua* spheres of recognition involve alienation.

7. In *Freedom's Right* (2014), Honneth rewrites Hegel's trinity of family, civil society and state as 'personal relations', 'market-economic action' and 'democratic will-formation' respectively.

8. One illustration of mutual recognition (by no means the only illustration) is that of a conversation in which no conversational partner dominates the other and where each has the equal opportunity to speak and to object and to disagree

or agree. In a 'good' conversation, no point or line of thought is excluded *a priori* and the exchange is open to all comers. Put another way, it is what Jürgen Habermas in his early – and radical – essay 'Wahrheitstheorien' (Habermas 1973: 211–65) means when he says that participants have an equal chance of performing 'speech acts of an unrestricted kind'. Only in an unrestricted conversation on a basis of equality, Habermas argues, can the 'truth' of a matter be found. In effect, Habermas restates Hegel's point that mutual recognition is the path to 'wisdom'. The radicality of this line of thought seems to have frightened even Habermas himself, who has since disowned it. For discussion, see McCarthy (1981: 300–8) and Gunn and Wilding (2013b).

9   For Honneth's use of the concept of *honour*, see Fraser and Honneth (2003: 139–40). For his use of the concept of *differentiation*, see Fraser and Honneth (2003: 138, 143, 184–5). Max Pensky (2011: 138) has drawn attention to the circumstance that 'Honneth like Habermas demonstrates his extreme indebtedness to the tradition of German philosophical sociology from Weber to Luhmann, wherein modernity is to be taken primarily as a process of differentiation'.

10 When this differentiation took place, 'members of the new type of society' became 'able to experience more aspects of their personality along the different models of recognition' (Fraser and Honneth 2003: 184).

11 Examples of such terms are 'refusal', 'inversion', 'rebellion' and 'resistance'. See the final section of this chapter.

12 For Marx's discussion of immanent critique (as distinct from external critique), see Marx and Engels (1975a: 270).

13 Ludwig Siep (2011) questions whether Honneth has 'perhaps over-estimated the immanent promise in the institutions he analyses'.

14 Ernst Bloch puts it pithily: 'the realm of freedom does not arrive with the gradual improvement in the quality of prison beds' (1980: 80).

15 The Social Democratic Party's manifesto lists its 'core values' as Freedom, Justice and Solidarity.

16 Our reference to institutions gives us a chance to anticipate a possible objection. The objection takes as its starting point the claim, raised by Habermas and subsequent Frankfurt School writers, that even in an emancipated society social institutions – most notably *law* and the attendant notion of *legal respect* – must obtain. In the light of this claim, is our own

invocation of 'revolutionary' recognition tinged with romanticism? Our response is that such an objection is wrong-headed. If social institutions are first introduced, uncontradicted recognition – or mutual recognition – cannot possibly be introduced at a later stage: such an attempt falls over its own feet. If, by contrast, mutual recognition is established as a priority and a sine qua non of emancipated existence, communities and individuals may address situations and exigencies as they (the communalizing individuals) see fit. As a limiting case, lead gauntlets may be donned to handle the radioactive material of social institutions but, unless mutual recognition is an absolute commitment, the overwhelming likelihood is that the gauntlets will never be taken off. The claim raised by Habermasian and post-Habermasian theorizing is grounded, we suggest, not in maturity of judgement but in conformity with the ways of a far-from-emancipated world.

Chapter 4

1 As Bonefeld and Tischler (2003: 2) put it, 'those who take the project of human emancipation seriously, will find little comfort in the idea that the party knows best. Contemporary anti-capitalism does well to keep clear of the Leninist conception of revolution.'

2 For discussion of recent uprisings, see, for example, Hancox 2011; Van Gelder 2011; Lunghi and Wheeler 2012; Marom and Klein 2012; Sitrin 2012; Döşemeci 2013; Graeber 2013; Oikonomakis and Roos 2013; Roos 2013; Della Porta 2015; Dinerstein 2015.

3 In interviews conducted with people who joined Occupy or became politicized by it, a common response is that the lack of hierarchy and the relative absence of sexism and racism were key motivations (for data, see Milkman, Luce and Lewis 2014). We note – more recently – the non-hierarchical, inclusive and alliance-building nature of the Black Lives Matter movement that re-emerged in 2020.

4 Occupy LSX was a case in point: occupiers faced the daunting prospect of targeting an institution – the London Stock Exchange – which lies on privatized land (indeed most of London's 'square mile', including parks, streets and pavements, belongs to the City of London Corporation). St Paul's Cathedral offered temporary 'sanctuary' to Occupy's tent city, but even the institutional power of the church met its match in capital.

5 In today's anti-capitalist struggles, the 'where' of revolution is likely not to be the factory but the city and everyday life itself. This was, perhaps, already the case in Marx's lifetime. When, famously, Marx describes the Paris Commune of 1871 as 'the glorious harbinger of a new society' (Marx and Engels 1986: 355) it seems he was thinking prefiguratively and with a citywide rather than simply a factory focus.

6 For this excellent phrase we are indebted to Robert C. Smith, erstwhile director of Heathwood Institute and Press.

7 For a critique of the entire discourse of human rights, see Gunn 1987.

8 Emma Goldman recalls interviewing Lenin in 1920 and his chilling reply to one of her questions: 'I informed him that I could not co-operate with a régime that persecuted anarchists or others for the sake of mere opinion. Moreover, there were even more appalling evils. How were we to reconcile them with the high goal he was aiming at. I mentioned some of them. His reply was that my attitude was bourgeois sentimentality. The proletarian dictatorship was engaged in a life-and-death struggle, and small considerations could not be permitted to weigh in the scale. Russia was making giant strides at home and abroad. It was igniting world revolution, and here I was lamenting over a little blood-letting. It was absurd and I must get over it' (Goldman 2006: 434).

9 The 'Nuit Debout' (Night Assembly) movement in France acknowledged this problem and sought a way round it. They held brief but regular, general-assembly type gatherings so as to avoid the 'burnout' associated with long-term occupation of urban space.

10 See, for example, Astra Taylor's recent book on democracy (Taylor 2019: Ch. 2). Taylor notes the bad faith of certain activists that can jeopardize mutual recognition – if one lets it. More optimistic is her discussion of the 'Rolling Jubilee' movement (Taylor 2019: Ch. 8) that emerged out of Occupy Wall Street, a movement which buys up student debt on the debt market (once its price has fallen due to non-payment) and writes it off. This, one could say, is a living example of mutual recognition: in writing off debt one removes, to use Marx's language (see Chapter 2), the debtor's 'humiliation', his or her 'servitude'.

11 Nancy Fraser calls Occupy's political stance 'conceptually incoherent' (Fraser 2013: 2–3). It is a stance that, she suggests, either 'presupposes that everyone can always act collectively on everything that concerns them' – something she describes as 'patently absurd' – or requires a decision-making council which is

itself 'an institutionalized power', that is, precisely what Occupy rejects. Whereas Occupy views democracy as requiring general assemblies, Fraser favours a 'two-track model' of democracy (Fraser 2013: 2) involving a decision-making council and a public. Which understanding is preferable? The revolutionary intent of Fraser's argument strikes us as vitiated by its deeply institutionalist tone. When Hegel (see Chapter 1) refers to institutions as 'spiritual masses', he underlines the quasi-natural inertia (and thence the alienation) that institutions possess. Institutions *stand over against* individuals – and *over-againstness*, pace Fraser, is a feature of any decision-making council's relationship to a public. To a public, a decision-making council could carry legitimacy only to the degree that it fully expresses their political will, which it cannot do without ceasing to be a body separate from the public itself. Political legitimacy, as Rousseau saw, is progressively lost to the degree that it is alienated from the people themselves (2012: Book III, Ch. 15). Rousseau's staunchest critic, Edmund Burke, was happy to defend this alienation: a representative, he argued, unable to consult his constituents on every issue, should decide what is in their interest: 'Your representative owes you, not his industry only, but his judgment; and he betrays, instead of serving you, if he sacrifices it to your opinion' (2009: 224). Fraser (we note) seems untroubled by this slippery slope inherent in representative democracy.

12 In Silke Helfrich's words, commoning is not 'a thing' but 'another way of being in the world'. For discussion of commoning in interactive terms, see Bollier and Helfrich 2015: 13–21.

13 If the typical figure of a worker has now become the immigrant, the itinerant and the refugee, as Federici (2019: 22) suggests, the picture changes. It changes still further when, elsewhere, Federici includes sex workers, indentured servants and peons in the workforce. A further set of considerations opens up once it is realized that precarious employment (in journalistic terms, 'the precariat') now covers around one-third of workers in developed Western economies. Precarious work transforms labour discipline into self-discipline, *self*-domination, as the residual security of employment rights is removed and the least insubordination can lead to dismissal. As labour, it is not just alienated but also an unrelenting source of worry. Linda Tirado's (2014) autobiography *Hand to Mouth* highlights in graphic ways a worry not just about how to make ends meet but also about how the several jobs typically needed to make a living can be timetabled and – particularly for women, caught up in a patriarchy that capital happily exploits – how the unpaid work of caring for family can be fitted in. Selma James (2012:

149) sums up this dilemma: 'capital takes who we could be and limits us to who we are. It takes our time, which happens to be our life. It takes us. We belong to it – not so different from the serf or the slave.'

14 A close study of recent social movements shows that the issue of 'demands' is a complex one. In the case of Occupy, there was a specific thinking behind the refusal to make them, one which follows consistently from the claim that we the people ('the 99 per cent') and not our parliamentary representatives (or the capitalist 1 per cent whose interests they reflect) are the ultimate political power. Moreover, so Occupiers have argued, why demand ad hoc policy changes to a society that is systematically unequal, oppressive and alienated? As Sarah van Gelder puts it, 'the system is broken in so many ways it's dizzying to try to name them all' (2011: 4).

15 See, for an introduction to her thought, Ostrom 2009. For a (sympathetic) discussion of her work, see Marshall 2008.

16 We emphasize that what we are setting forth is not a notion of revolutionary *purity*. Mutual recognition is precisely *not* the life of a 'beautiful soul' – to use the term with which Hegel lampooned the refusal to make moral compromises (see 1977: 383f). Our point is simply that when a core principle is not held in view and sustained in a living way, instrumental reasoning and action come all too easily into play.

17 For Guy Debord (who we quoted in Chapter 1), 'the organisational question became the weakest aspect of radical theory, a confused terrain lending itself to the revival of hierarchical and statist tactics borrowed from the bourgeois revolution' (1987: 46).

18 The philosopher Ivan Illich would always keep a candle on his table. He explained, 'Our conversation should always go on with the certainty that there is someone else who will knock at the door, and the candle stands for him or her. It is a constant reminder that the community is never closed' (2005: 105–51).

Chapter 5

1 If we have a disagreement with Bookchin, it is over his idea of 'communalist institutions' as a counter-power to the state and capital (see, for example,

2015: 24, 35, 45, 48, 51, 62). Our argument in this book has been that *all* forms of 'institution', whether capitalist, socialist or 'communalist', contradict recognition. Mutual recognition is the unconstrained practice of freedom; once institutionalized it ceases to be what it is.

2 Our use of the term 'nature' calls for comment. Authors such as McKibben (2006), Moore (2015) and Vogel (1996) argue that the term should be abandoned. For McKibben and particularly for Vogel, this is because, so they argue, there is nothing now untouched by human civilization. All nature has become 'second nature' (Vogel 1996: 35). For Moore, it is because everything that exists on the planet is a 'bundle' of 'the human' and 'the non-human' (2015: 27). We do not explore these views here (for a critique, see Malm 2018: Ch. 2) but note a problem with each of them. Marx (following Hegel) tells us that a relation of *mediation* exists between human activity and the non-human world. That the non-human world is mediated by human activity does not, however, mean that the former is abstractly *negated*; nor can a relationship of mediation be grasped as mere *admixture*.

3 The line comes from Marx's critique of Feuerbach. Dispute over the abstract universal 'Man' was a recurring theme for the Young Hegelians: while some, such as Feuerbach and Stiner, wielded the category in iconoclastic fashion, others, such as Marx and Hess, sought to break it down into its antagonistic parts.

4 In 1969, Herbert Marcuse wrote of the need to 'change the concept of revolution' so as to 'break with the continuity of the technical apparatus of productivity which, for Marx, would extend (freed from capitalist abuse) to the socialist society. Such "technological" continuity would constitute a fateful link between capitalism and socialism, because this technical apparatus has, in its very structure and scope, become an apparatus of control and domination. *Cutting this link* would mean, not to regress in technical progress, but to reconstruct the technical apparatus in accordance with the needs of free men, guided by their own consciousness and sensibility, by their autonomy' (2014: 205, emphasis in original).

5 As an aside, we note how much has now been written on Marx as ecologist, yet how little has been written on Hegel's contribution to the topic. In his early writings Hegel anticipates ecological thinking, describing labour as 'the putting of the [natural object] to death, ripping it out of its living context', a subjugation of the natural world for which humans pay a high price: 'what [man] gains from nature, the more he subdues it, the lower he sinks himself' (1979: 247).

6 What would remain instead might resemble the grim tableau of Beckett's *Endgame*, where the tragicomic misrecognition between the characters has an analogue in the moribund nature onto which they gaze. In Adorno's interpretation of Beckett's play, some unnamed catastrophe has desolated the planet, reducing society to its last men and nature to a corpse. The Hegelian struggle of master and slave for freedom has reverted to a natural struggle for survival, in the farcical form of two bickering senile clowns. The drama of master and slave, Adorno suggests, has reached a nadir in a stage unforeseeable by Hegel himself: the oppressed have been so thoroughly beaten down that they no longer have the power to grasp their chains and overthrow their oppressor (Adorno 1999: 250). In the morass of mutual unfreedom, Adorno tells us, the pendulum of struggle stops and history peters out. Beckett and Adorno, we suggest, warn us of one possible 'end' of history.

7 Mann and Wainwright's book was written before the Corona pandemic, as was ours. Nevertheless, we suggest that the danger of a 'Climate Leviathan' which uses environmental risks to justify the policing of everyday life through emergency measures has only been underlined by recent events.

8 We note, by way of example, that the site of the Diggers' communist experiment at St George's Hill, Surrey, is now a gated community.

9 In John Lanchester's dystopian climate change novel *The Wall* there is a moment when the tables of domination are turned and the protagonist from the (unnamed) rich nation suddenly sees through the other's (the refugee's) eyes. 'I'd been brought up not to think about the Others in terms of where they came from or who they were, to ignore all that – they were just Others. But maybe, now that I was one of them, they weren't Others any more. If I was an Other and they were Others perhaps none of us were Others but instead we were a new Us' (2019: 203).

10 To state Locke's position in more technical terms, Locke draws upon Samuel Pufendorf's *Of the Law of Nature and Nation*'s notion of a 'negative community of goods' (1934: Book IV, Ch. IV) that envisages individuals in a state of nature as carving out their own portions of nature as a common stock and owning this portion as their private property. The modern natural law tradition, to which Pufendorf and Locke belong, was the most energetic transmitter of ideas about property in early modern thought.

11 Have we made a case for Marx's relevance for green thought? A green critic of Marx's argument may still be unsatisfied. They may point to the coda to the quote from *Capital* and ask, isn't Marx's phrase 'boni patres familias' (good

heads of the household) evidence of an anthropocentric – even patriarchal (*patres familias*) – attitude towards the non-human world? Our reply is that this might only be the case if the familial duty of care which Marx likens to care for nature is necessarily patriarchal. But Marx clearly did not think in this way, as we know from his trenchant critique of the bourgeois nuclear family, a critique which, in the twentieth century, inspired a host of experiments in different ways of conducting relationships of love and child-rearing. What if the caregiving traditionally offered by the family were not arranged in a hierarchical and role-defined way? It is interesting that Marx speaks of 'heads' (*patres*) and not a 'head' (*pater*) of this family. His choice of words suggests he is thinking of a more communal, collective way of arranging our duty of care for the environment and for generations to come.

12 William Clare Roberts gives a twist to the orthodox Marxist idea that capitalism is a 'precondition' for communism: 'the power developed by capitalism is the power to destroy workers' lives, to expose large swaths of humanity to immiseration and sudden desolation, and to undermine the earth's capacity to sustain us all. The development of this power of destruction is, nonetheless, the development of the material conditions of communism, for the simple reason that capitalism gives to the laboring class a powerful motive to cooperate in the construction of a new society. It does so, on the one hand, by destroying the laborers' capacity for going it alone, and, on the other, by creating disasters so immense in scale that only massive collective efforts could possibly address them' (2017: 171).

13 On indigenous ecosocialist activism, particularly the ideas of the Zapatista-inspired Hugo Blanco, see Wall (2018). On Chico Mendes and the struggle for the Brazilian rainforest, see Löwy (2015: Ch. 4). On indigenous struggles in Peru, Ecuador and Bolivia, see Löwy (2015: Ch. 5). On the First Nations struggles in North America, see Klein (2015: Ch. 11) and Klein (2017: Ch. 12).

14 Marx is under no illusions that full mutual recognition exists among the Iroqouis. As Dunayevskaya notes, women's roles there are still in many respects subordinate and subject to a division of labour and there remains 'the antagonistic relationship between the chief and the masses' (1981: 182). Yet Marx's admiration clearly stems from the stark contrast the Iroquois represent to capitalist society.

15 Silvia Federici writes, 'When we speak of commons, then, we do not only speak of one particular reality or a set of small-scale experiments. . . . We speak of

large-scale social formations that at times were continent-wide, like the networks of commons that in precolonial America stretched from present-day Chile to Nicaragua and Texas, connected by a vast array of exchanges, including gift and barter' (2019: 87). For debate on Federici's notion of the commons, see Barbagallo, Beuret and Harvie (2019).

16 Bookchin (1980: 76) cites the research of anthropologist Dorothy Lee into the Wintu people, who for centuries (perhaps millennia) have inhabited what is now Northern California. The Wintu lack any word for 'have' to describe their relationship to the things around them; instead they say they 'live with' these things. The absence of a proprietorial relationship towards nature expresses itself at the fundamental level of grammar and syntax. Like so many other First Nations, the Wintu suffered horrifically at the hands of settler colonists.

17 In her novel *The Dispossessed*, Ursula Le Guin writes that the political philosopher Odo based her plan for an anarchist utopia 'on the generous ground of Urras'. But 'on arid Anarres, the communities had to scatter widely in search of resources' (1999: 82). Le Guin in effect points to the issue of mutual recognition's 'environment'.

18 It is in this sense that the authors in the recent volume of *Open Marxism* (Dinerstein et al. 2019: 1) 'write against a closing of the world'.

REFERENCES

Adorno, T. (1978), *Minima Moralia*, trans. E. Jephcott, London: Verso.
Adorno, T. (1993), *Hegel: Three Studies*, trans. S. Weber Nicholson, Cambridge, MA and London: MIT Press.
Adorno, T. (1999), *Aesthetic Theory*, trans. R. Hullot-Kentor, London: Athlone.
Althusser, L. and Balibar, E. (1970), *Reading Capital*, London: New Left Books.
Anderson, S. (2009), *Hegel's Theory of Recognition*, New York: Continuum.
Angus, I. (2016), *Facing the Anthropocene: Fossil Capitalism and the Crisis of the Earth System*, New York: Monthly Review Press.
Arendt, H. (1975), 'Sonning Prize Speech', Copenhagen, 18 April 1975, https://memory.loc.gov/cgi-bin/ampage?collId=mharendt_pub&fileName=05/052270/052270page.db&recNum=12 (accessed 15 December 2019).
Barbagallo, C., Beuret, N. and Harvie, D. eds (2019), *Commoning With George Caffentzis and Silvia Federici*, London: Pluto Press.
Bedorf, T. (2010), *Verkennende Anerkennung: Über Identität und Politik*, Frankfurt: Suhrkamp.
Beiser, F. (2005), *Hegel*, London: Routledge.
Bellamy Foster, J. (2000), *Marx's Ecology: Materialism and Nature*, New York: Monthly Review Press.
Benjamin, W. (1969), *Illuminations*, trans. H. Zohn, New York: Schocken.
Benjamin, W. (1998), *Understanding Brecht*, trans. A. Bostock, London: Verso.
Berlin, I. (2006), 'Two Concepts of Liberty', in D. Miller (ed.), *The Liberty Reader*, 33–57, Edinburgh: Edinburgh University Press.
Bloch, E. (1970), *Man on His Own*, trans. E. Ashton, New York: Herder and Herder.
Bloch, E. (1971), *On Karl Marx*, trans. J. Maxwell, New York: Herder & Herder.
Bloch, E. (1980), *Abschied von der Utopie*, ed. H. Gekle, Frankfurt: Suhrkamp.
Bloch, E. (2006), *Traces*, trans. A. Nassar, Redwood: Stanford University Press.
Bollier, D. and Helfrich, S., eds (2015), *Patterns of Commoning*, Amherst: Commons Strategies Group.
Bonefeld, W. and Tischler, S. (2003), *What Is to be Done? Leninism, Anti-Leninist Marxism and the Question of Revolution Today*, Farnham: Ashgate.
Bookchin, M. (1980), *Toward an Ecological Society*, Montreal and New York: Black Rose Books.

Bookchin, M. (1993), 'Society and Ecology', http://social-ecology.org/wp/1993/01/society-and-ecology/ (accessed 3 January 2020).

Bookchin, M. (2015), *The Next Revolution: Popular Assemblies and the Promise of Direct Democracy*, London: Verso.

Buck-Morss, S. (2009), *Hegel, Haiti and Universal History*, Pennsylvania: University of Pittsburgh Press.

Burke, E. (2009), *Selected Writings and Speeches*, New Brunswick: Transaction Publishers.

Caffentzis, G. (2013), *In Letters of Blood and Fire: Work, Machines, and the Crisis of Capitalism*, Brooklyn and Oakland: Common Notions / PM Press.

Chandler, R. (1951), *The High Window*, Harmondsworth: Penguin.

Chitty, A. (1998), 'Recognition and Relations of Production', *Historical Materialism* 2, no. 1: 57–98.

Chomsky, N. (2016), 'An Interview with Noam Chomsky', *The Colossus*, 1 June 2016, https://chomsky.info/06012016/ (accessed 18 December 2019).

Cleaver, H. (2000), *Reading Capital Politically (2nd edition)*, Leeds and Edinburgh: Antithesis/AK Press.

Cleaver, H. (2017), *Rupturing the Dialectic*, Oakland: P. M. Press.

Commune (2019), 'No Way Out but Through', *Commune Mag*, no. 4, Fall 2019, https://communemag.com/issue/fall-2019/ (accessed 4 December 2019).

Dangl, B. (2011), *Dancing With Dynamite: Social Movements and States in Latin America*, Oakland and Edinburgh: AK Press.

Davis, A. (2012), *The Meaning of Freedom*, San Francisco: City Lights Books.

De Angelis, M. (2017), *Omnia Sunt Communia: On the Commons and the Transformation to Postcapitalism*, London: Zed Books.

De Beauvoir, S. (1956), *The Second Sex*, trans. H. Parshley, London: Jonathan Cape.

Debord, G. (1987), *Society of the Spectacle*, trans. K. Knabb, London: Rebel Press.

Della Porta, D. (2015), *Social Movements in Times of Austerity: Bringing Capitalism Back into Protest Analysis*, Cambridge: Polity.

Della Porta, D., ed. (2017), *Solidarity Mobilizations in the 'Refugee Crisis'*, London: Palgrave Macmillan.

Deranty, J.-P. (2004), 'Injustice, Violence and Social Struggle: The Critical Potential of Axel Honneth's Theory of Recognition', *Critical Horizons* 5, no. 1: 297–322.

Dinerstein, A. (2015), *The Politics of Autonomy in Latin America: The Art of Organising Hope*, London: Palgrave Macmillan.

Dinerstein, A., García Vela, A., González, E. and Holloway, J. (2019), *Open Marxism 4: Against a Closing World*, London: Pluto Press.

Döşemeci, M. (2013), 'Don't Move, Occupy! Social Movement vs Social Arrest', *Roar Magazine*, 5 November 2013, https://roarmag.org/essays/occupy-revolution-mehmet-dosemeci/ (accessed 19 October 2019).

Dunayevskaya, R. (1981), *Rosa Luxemburg, Women's Liberation, and Marx's Philosophy of Revolution*, Sussex: Harvester Press.

Dunayevskaya, R. (2012), *The Dunayevskaya-Marcuse-Fromm Correspondence, 1954–1978: Dialogues on Hegel, Marx, and Critical Theory*, ed. K. Anderson and R. Rockwell, Plymouth: Lexington Books.

Ehrenreich, B. (2019a), 'Climate Change Is Here—and It Looks Like Starvation', *The Nation*, 1 March 2019, https://www.thenation.com/article/climate-change-media-humanitarian-crises/ (accessed 7 December 2019).

Ehrenreich, B. (2019b), 'Sea of Troubles: Inside the Effort to Rescue Europe's Unwelcome Immigrants', *The New Republic*, 17 October 2019, https://newrepublic.com/article/155271/europe-migrant-crisis-mediterranean-rescue-boat-alan-kurdi (accessed 5 December 2019).

Emcke, C. (2000), 'Between Choice and Coercion: Identities, Injuries and Different Forms of Recognition', *Constellations* 7, no. 4: 483–95.

Engels, F. (1946), *Ludwig Feuerbach and the End of Classical German Philosophy*, Moscow: Progress Publishers.

Engels, F. (1959), *Anti-Dühring*, Moscow: Progress Publishers.

Fanon, F. (2007), *Black Skin, White Masks*, trans. R. Philcox, New York: Grove Press.

Federici, S. (2008), *Revolution at Point Zero*, Oakland: PM Press.

Federici, S. (2019), *Re-enchanting the World*, Oakland: PM Press.

Feuerbach, L. (1966), *Principles of the Philosophy of the Future*, trans. M. Vogel, Indianapolis: Bobbs-Merrill.

Fichte, J. G. (2000), *Foundations of Natural Right*, trans. M. Bauer, Cambridge: Cambridge University Press.

Flaubert, G. (1964), *Sentimental Education*, Harmondsworth: Penguin.

Flickinger, Hans-Georg (2008), 'Die Anfänge der Hegelschen Anerkennungstheorie', in W. Schmied-Kowarzik and H. Eidam (eds), *Anfänge bei Hegel*, 93–107, Kassel: Kassel University Press.

Fraser, N. (1997), 'Rejoinder to Iris Young', *New Left Review*, no. 223: 126–9.

Fraser, N. (2013), 'Against Anarchism', *Public Seminar*, www.publicseminar.org/2013/10/against-anarchism/#.Vdefy0V41UU (accessed 19 October 2019).

Fraser, N. and Honneth, A. (2003), *Redistribution or Recognition?* London: Verso.

Goldman, E. (2006), *Living My Life*, London: Penguin.

Graeber, D. (2013), *The Democracy Project: A History, A Crisis, A Movement*, London: Allen Lane.

Graeber, D. (n.d.), 'Some Remarks on Consensus', Occupy Wall Street, http://occupywallstreet.net/story/some-remarks-consensus (accessed 19 October 2019).

Grollios, V. (2017), *Negativity and Democracy: Marxism and the Critical Theory Tradition*, London: Routledge.

Gunn, R. (1987), 'Rights', *Edinburgh Review*, no. 77, May 1987, http://www.richard-gunn.com/marx-and-marxism/ (accessed 9 December 2019).

Gunn, R. (2015), *Lo que usted siempre quiso saber sobre Hegel y no se atrevió a preguntar*, Buenos Aires: Ediciones Herramienta.

Gunn, R. and Wilding, A. (2012), 'Holloway, La Boétie, Hegel', *Journal of Classical Sociology* 12, Issue 2 (Special Issue on John Holloway's *Crack Capitalism*).

Gunn, R. and Wilding, A. (2013a), 'Revolutionary or Less-than-Revolutionary Recognition?', http://www.richard-gunn.com/hegel/ (accessed 4 December 2019).

Gunn, R. and Wilding, A. (2013b), 'Is the Frankfurt School Still Relevant?', http://www.richard-gunn.com/marx-and-marxism/ (accessed 4 December 2019).

Gunn, R. and Wilding, A. (2014a), 'Recognition Contradicted', *South Atlantic Quarterly* 113 (Spring 2014): 339–52.

Gunn, R. and Wilding, A. (2014b), 'Marx and Recognition', http://www.richard-gunn.com/marx-and-marxism/ (accessed 27 November 2019).

Gunn, R., Wilding, A., Smith, R. C., Fuchs, C. and Ott, M. (2015), 'Occupy and Prefiguration: A Roundtable Discussion', http://www.richard-gunn.com/politics/ (accessed 27 November 2019).

Habermas, J. (1973), 'Wahrheitstheorien', in H. Fahrenbach (ed.), *Wirklichkeit und Reflexion*, 211–65, Pfullingen: Neske.

Hamsun, K. (2016), *Hunger*, trans. S. Lyngstad, Edinburgh: Canongate.

Hancox, D., ed. (2011), *Fight Back! A Reader on the Winter of Protest*, London: Open Democracy.

Hardin, G. (1968), 'The Tragedy of the Commons', *Science* 162, no. 3859: 1243–8.

Hardt, M. and Negri, A. (2012), *Declaration*, New York: Argo.

Harvey, D. (2013), *Rebel Cities*, London: Verso.

Hegel, G. W. F. (1956), *The Philosophy of History*, trans. J. Sibree, New York: Dover Publications.

Hegel, G. W. F. (1970), *Werke in zwanzig Bänden*, Bd. 3: *Phänomenologie des Geistes*, ed. E. Moldenhauer and K. M. Michel, Frankfurt am Main: Suhrkamp.

Hegel, G. W. F. (1977), *Phenomenology of Spirit*, trans. A.V. Miller, Oxford: Clarendon Press.

Hegel, G. W. F. (1979), *System of Ethical Life and First Philosophy of Spirit*, trans. H. S. Harris and T. M. Knox, Albany: SUNY Press.

Hegel, G. W. F. (1983), *Philosophie des Rechts : die Vorlesung von 1819/20 in einer Nachschrift*, ed. D. Henrich, Frankfurt: Suhrkamp.

Hegel, G. W. F. (1988), *The Difference between Fichte's and Schelling's Systems of Philosophy*, trans. H. S. Harris and W. Cerf, Albany: SUNY Press.

Hegel, G. W. F. (2008), *The Philosophy of Right*, trans. T. M. Knox, revised by S. Houlgate, Oxford: Oxford University Press.

Hess, M. (2004), *The Holy History of Mankind and Other Writings*, ed. S. Avineri, Cambridge: Cambridge University Press.

Hill, C. (1975), *The World Turned Upside Down*, Harmondsworth: Penguin

Holloway, J. (2005), *Change the World Without Taking Power*, London: Pluto Press.

Holloway, J. (2010), *Crack Capitalism*, London: Pluto Press.

Holloway, J. (2015), 'Read *Capital*: The First Sentence', *Historical Materialism* 23, no. 3: 3–26.

Holloway, J. (2016), *In, Against and Beyond Capitalism: The San Francisco Lectures*, Oakland: PM Press.

Honneth, A. (1995), *The Struggle for Recognition*, trans. J. Anderson, Cambridge: Polity Press.

Honneth, A. (2005), 'Between Aristotle and Kant – Sketch for a Morality of Recognition', in W. Edelstein and G. Nunner-Winkler (eds), *Morality in Context*, 41–56, Amsterdam: Elsevier.

Honneth, A. (2007), 'Recognition as Ideology', in B. van den Brink and D. Owen (eds), *Recognition and Power*, 323–47, Cambridge: Cambridge University Press.

Honneth, A. (2010), *The Pathologies of Individual Freedom*, trans. L. Löb, Princeton: Princeton University Press.

Honneth, A. (2012), *The I in We*, trans. J. Ganahl, Cambridge: Polity Press.

Honneth, A. (2013), 'Recognition and Critical Theory Today: An Interview with Axel Honneth', *Philosophy and Social Criticism* 39, no. 2: 209–21.

Honneth, A. (2014), *Freedom's Right*, trans. J. Ganahl, Cambridge: Polity Press.

Honneth, A. (2015), *Die Idee des Sozialismus: Versuch einer Aktualisierung*, Frankfurt: Suhrkamp.

Honneth, A. (2016), 'On the Poverty of Our Liberty: The Greatness and Limits of Hegel's Doctrine of Ethical Life', in K. Genel and J.-P. Deranty (eds), *Recognition or Disagreement*, 156–76, New York: Columbia University Press.

Honneth, A. (2018), *Anerkennung: Eine europäische Ideengeschichte*, Frankfurt: Suhrkamp.

Hook, S. (1962), *From Hegel to Marx*, Ann Arbor: University of Michigan Press.

Horkheimer, M. (1969), 'Max Horkheimer on Critical Theory', https://www.youtube.com/watch?v=OBaY09Qi-w0#t=49 (accessed 18 December 2019).

Horkheimer, M. (1972), *Critical Theory: Selected Essays*, trans. M. O'Connell and others, New York: Seabury Press.

Horkheimer, M. and Adorno, T. (2002), *Dialectic of Enlightenment*, trans. G. Schmid Noerr and E. Jephcott, Redwood: Stanford University Press.

Illich, I. (2005), *The Rivers North of the Future: The Testament of Ivan Illich*, Toronto: House of Anansi Press.

James, S. (2012), *Sex, Race, and Class: A Selection of Writings, 1952–2011*, Oakland: PM Press.

Klein, N. (2015), *This Changes Everything: Capitalism vs. the Climate*, London: Penguin

Klein, N. (2017), *No Is Not Enough: Defeating the New Shock Politics*, London: Allen Lane.

Kojève, A. (1969), *Introduction to the Reading of Hegel*, trans. J. Nichols, New York: Basic Books.

Lanchester, J. (2019), *The Wall*, London: Faber & Faber.

Lazzarato, M. (2011), *The Making of Indebted Man*, Amsterdam: Semiotexte.

Le Guin, U. (1999), *The Dispossessed*, London: Millenium.

Lenin, V. (1969), *Selected Works, Volume 2*, London: Lawrence and Wishart.

Linebaugh, P. (2019), *Red Round Globe Hot Burning*, Oakland: California University Press.

Linebaugh, P. and Rediker, M. (2013), *The Many-Headed Hydra: Sailors, Slaves, Commoners, and the Hidden History of the Revolutionary Atlantic*, 2nd edn, Boston: Beacon Press.

Locke, J. (1986), *Two Treatises of Government*, London: Dent.

Löwy, M. (2015), *Ecosocialism: A Radical Alternative to Capitalist Catastrophe*, Chicago: Haymarket.

Lukács, G. (1975), *The Young Hegel*, trans. R. Livingstone, London: Merlin Press.

Lunghi, A. and Wheeler, S., eds (2012), *Occupy Everything*, Wivenhoe: Minor Compositions.

Luxemburg, R. (1961), *The Russian Revolution and Leninism or Marxism?* Ann Arbor: University of Michigan Press.

Luxemburg, R. (2004), *The Rosa Luxemburg Reader*, ed. P. Hudis and K. Anderson, New York: Monthly Review Press.

MacPherson, C. (1962), *The Political Theory of Possessive Individualism*, Oxford: Oxford University Press.

Malm, A. (2016), *Fossil Capital: The Rise of Steam Power and the Roots of Global Warming*, London: Verso.

Malm, A. (2018), *The Progress of This Storm: Nature and Society in a Warming World*, London: Verso.

Mann, G. and Wainwright, J. (2018), *Climate Leviathan: A Political Theory of Our Planetary Future*, London: Verso.

Marcuse, H. (1968), *One Dimensional Man*, London: Sphere Books.

Marcuse, H. (2014), *Collected Papers of Herbert Marcuse, Vol. 6: Marxism, Revolution and Utopia*, ed. D. Kellner and C. Pierce, London and New York: Routledge.

Markell, P. (2000), 'The Recognition of Politics: A Comment on Emcke and Tully', *Constellations* 7, no. 4: 496–506.

Markell, P. (2003), *Bound by Recognition*, Princeton: Princeton University Press.

Marom, Y. and Klein, N. (2012), 'Why Now? What Next? A Conversation about Occupy Wall Street', *The Nation*, 9 January, https://www.thenation.com/article/why-now-whats-next-naomi-klein-and-yotam-marom-conversation-about-occupy-wall-street/ (accessed 4 December 2019).

Marshall, G. (2008), 'Nesting, Subsidiarity and Community-Based Environmental Governance Beyond the Local Level', *International Journal of the Commons* 2, no. 1: 75–97.

Marx, K. (1971), *A Contribution to the Critique of Political Economy*, trans. S. Ryazanskaya, London: Lawrence and Wishart.

Marx, K. (1973), *Grundrisse*, trans. M. Nicolaus, Harmondsworth: Penguin.

Marx, K. (1974), *Ethnological Notebooks*, ed. L. Krader, Assen: Van Gorcum.

Marx, K. (1975), *Kapital* Bd. I in Marx & Engels *Werke, Vol. 23*, Berlin: Dietz Verlag.

Marx, K. (1976), *Capital* Vol. 1, trans. B. Fowkes, Harmondsworth: Penguin.

Marx, K. (1981), *Capital* Vol. 3, trans. D. Fernbach, Harmondsworth: Penguin.

Marx, K. (1992), *Early Writings*, trans. R. Livingstone and G. Benton, Harmondsworth: Penguin.

Marx, K. and Engels, F. (1967), *The Communist Manifesto*, Harmondsworth: Penguin.

Marx, K. and Engels, F. (1975a), *Collected Works Vol 3*, London: Lawrence and Wishart.

Marx, K. and Engels, F. (1975b), *Collected Works Vol 4*, London: Lawrence and Wishart.

Marx, K. and Engels, F. (1976a), *Collected Works Vol 5*, London: Lawrence and Wishart.

Marx, K. and Engels, F. (1976b), *Collected Works Vol. 6*, London: Lawrence and Wishart.

Marx, K. and Engels, F. (1978), *Collected Works Vol. 10*, London: Lawrence and Wishart.

Marx, K. and Engels, F. (1986), *Collected Works Vol. 22*, London: Lawrence and Wishart.

Marx, K. and Engels, F. (1987a), *Collected Works Vol. 25*, London: Lawrence and Wishart.

Marx, K. and Engels, F. (1987b), *Collected Works Vol. 42*, London: Lawrence and Wishart.

McCarthy, T. (1981), *The Critical Theory of Jürgen Habermas*, Cambridge, MA and London: MIT Press.

McKibben, B. (2006), *The End of Nature*, New York: Random House.

McLellan, D. (1980), *The Young Hegelians and Karl Marx*, London: Macmillan.

Milkman, R., Luce, S. and Lewis, P. (2014), 'Occupy Wall Street', in Jeff Goodwin and James L. Jasper, *The Social Movements Reader: Cases and Concepts*, 30–44, Oxford: Wiley.

Monahan, M. (2006), 'Recognition Beyond Struggle: On a Liberatory Account of Hegelian Recognition', *Social Theory and Practice* 32, no. 3: 389–414.

Moore, J. (2015), *Capitalism in the Web of Life: Ecology and the Accumulation of Capital*, London: Verso.

Öcalan, A. (2011), *Democratic Confederalism*, London: Transmedia Publishing.

Öcalan, A. (2019), *The Sociology of Freedom: Manifesto of the Democratic Civilization, Volume III*, Oakland: PM Press.

Oikonomakis, L. and Roos, J. (2013), '"Que No Nos Representan": The Crisis of Representation and the Resonance of the Real Democracy Movement from the Indignados to Occupy', https://roarmag.org/wp-content/uploads/2013/0 2/Resonance-Real-Democracy-Movement-Indignados-Occupy.pdf (accessed 19 December 2019).

Ostrom, E. (2009), 'Beyond Markets and States: Polycentric Governance of Complex Economic Systems' (Nobel Prize lecture 8 December 2009), https://www.nobelpri ze.org/prizes/economic-sciences/2009/ostrom/lecture/ (accessed 2 November 2019).

Pannekoek, A. (1948), 'Revolt of the Scientists', *Retort* 4, no. 2: 19–23.

Pensky, M. (2011), 'Social Solidarity and Intersubjective Recognition: On Axel Honneth's *Struggle for Recognition*', in D. Petherbridge (ed.), *Axel Honneth: Critical Essays*, 125–53, Leiden: Brill.

Pippin, R. (2000), 'What Is the Question for which Hegel's Theory of Recognition is the Answer?' *European Journal of Philosophy* 8, no. 2: 155–72.

Postone, M. (1993), *Time, Labour and Social Domination: A Reinterpretation of Marx's Critical Theory*, Cambridge: Cambridge University Press.

Pufendorf, S. (1934), *The Law of Nature and Nation*, trans. C. Oldfather and W. Oldfather, Oxford: Clarendon Press.

Rauch, L. (1983), *Hegel and the Human Spirit*, Detroit: Wayne University Press.

Reichelt, H. (2005), 'Social Reality as Appearance: Some Notes on Marx's Conception of Reality', in W. Bonefeld and K. Psychopedis (eds), *Human Dignity: Social Autonomy and the Critique of Capitalism*, 31–67, Farnham, Ashgate.

Renault, E. (2011), 'The Theory of Recognition and Critique of Institutions', in D. Danielle Petherbridge (ed.), *Axel Honneth: Critical Essays*, 207–31, Leiden: Brill.

Renault, E. (2012), 'The Early Marx and Hegel: The Young-Hegelian Mediation', https://marxandphilosophy.org.uk/wp-content/uploads/2018/01/renault2012.doc (accessed 3 October 2019).

Renault, E. (2013), 'Three Marxian Approaches to Recognition', *Ethical Theory and Moral Practice* 16, no. 4: 699–791.

Roberts, W. (2017), *Marx's Inferno: The Political Theory of Capital*, Princeton and Oxford: Princeton University Press.

Roos, J. (2013), 'Autonomy: An Idea whose Time Has Come', *ROAR Magazine*, 23 June 2013.

Rosemont, F. (1989), 'Karl Marx and the Iroquois', https://libcom.org/library/karl-marx-iroquois-franklin-rosemont (accessed 4 January 2020).

Ross, K. (2018), 'Against Commemoration: Unearthing the Lives and Afterlives of May '68', http://www.threadjournal.org/issue-one/an-interview-with-kristin-ross/ (accessed 21 November 2019).

Rousseau, J.-J. (1984), *A Discourse on Inequality*, Harmondsworth: Penguin.

Rousseau, J.-J. (2012), *The Social Contract and Other Political Writings*, trans. Q. Hoare, Harmondsworth: Penguin.

Rowbotham, S. Segal, L. and Wainwright, H. (1979), *Beyond the Fragments*, London: Merlin Press.

Rubio-Pueyo, V. (2017), 'Municipalism in Spain', Rosa Luxemburg Stiftung, http://www.rosalux-nyc.org/wp-content/files_mf/rubiopueyo_eng.pdf (accessed 22 November 2019).

Rude, G. (1959), *The Crowd in the French Revolution*, Oxford: Oxford University Press.

Saito, K. (2017), *Karl Marx's Ecosocialism*, New York: Monthly Review Press.

Sartre, J.-P. (2003), *Being and Nothingness*, trans. H. Barnes, London: Routledge.

Sartre, J.-P. (2004), *Critique of Dialectical Reason*, trans. Q. Hoare, London: Verso.

Sartre, J.-P. (2007), *Existentialism is a Humanism*, trans. A. Cohen-Solal, New Haven and London: Yale University Press.

Schmidt, A. (1971), *The Concept of Nature in Marx*, trans. B. Fowkes, London: New Left Books.

Siep, L. (2011), 'Pessimistisches Resümee trennt Honneth von Hegel', *Die Zeit*, 18 August 2011.

Singer, P. (2011), *Practical Ethics*, 3rd edn, Cambridge: Cambridge University Press.
Sitrin, M. (2012), *Everyday Revolutions: Horizontalism and Autonomy in Argentina*, London: Zed Books.
Smith, A. (1979), *An Inquiry into the Nature and Causes of the Wealth of Nations*, Indianapolis: Liberty Fund (reprint of OUP edn).
Smith, N., ed. (1984), *A Collection of Ranter Writings from the Seventeenth Century*, London: Junction Books.
Stepelevich, L. S., ed. (1983), *The Young Hegelians: An Anthology*, Cambridge: Cambridge University Press.
Stirner, M. (1915), *The Ego and His Own*, London, A.C. Fifield.
Taylor, A. (2019), *Democracy May Not Exist but We'll Miss It When It's Gone*, New York: Metropolitan Books.
Taylor, C. (1994), 'The Politics of Recognition', in A. Gutman (ed.), *Multiculturalism*, 25–73, Princeton: Princeton University Press.
Thompson, E. P. (1993), *Customs in Common*, Harmondsworth: Penguin.
Thompson, S. (2006), *The Political Theory of Recognition*, Cambridge: Polity Press.
Tirado, L. (2014), *Hand to Mouth: The Truth about Being Poor in a Wealthy World*, London: Virago.
Toews, J. E. (1980), *Hegelianism*, Cambridge: Cambridge University Press.
Tully, J. (1999), 'The Agonic Freedom of Citizens', *Economy and Society* 28, no. 2: 161–82.
Tully, J. (2000), 'Struggles Over Recognition and Distribution', *Constellations* 7, no. 4: 469–82.
Tully, J. (2004), 'Recognition and Dialogue: The Emergence of a New Field', *Critical Review of International Social and Political Philosophy* 7, no. 3: 84–106.
Van Gelder, S., ed. (2011), *This Changes Everything: Occupy Wall Street and the 99% Movement*, Oakland: Berrett-Koehler.
Vogel, S. (1996), *Against Nature: The Concept of Nature in Critical Theory*, New York: SUNY Press.
Wall, D. (2014), *The Commons in History: Culture, Conflict and Ecology*, Cambridge, MA and London: MIT Press.
Wall, D. (2018), *Hugo Blanco: A Revolutionary for Life*, London: Merlin Press and Resistance Books.
Wallace-Wells, D. (2018), *The Uninhabitable Earth: Life After Warming*, New York: Tim Duggan Books.
Wilding, A. (2008), 'Ideas for a Critical Theory of Nature', *Capitalism, Nature, Socialism* 19, no. 4: 48–67.

Williams, R. (1997), *Hegel's Ethics of Recognition*, Berkeley: University of California Press.

Winnicott, D. (1990), *The Maturational Processes and the Facilitating Environment*, London: Karnac Books.

Winstanley, G. (1973), *The Law of Freedom and Other Writings*, ed. C. Hill, Harmondsworth: Penguin.

Woodhouse, A. (1992), *Puritanism and Liberty*, London: J.M. Dent.

Wright, E. O. (1976), 'Class Boundaries in Advanced Capitalist Societies', *New Left Review*, no. 98: 3–41.

Zibechi, R. (2010), *Dispersing Power*, Oakland and Edinburgh: AK Press.

Zibechi, R. (2012), *Territories in Resistance*, Oakland and Edinburgh: AK Press.

NAME & SUBJECT INDEX

Adorno, T. W.   69, 81, 115, 143 n.9, 144 n.13, 156 n.6
alienation   1, 13–14, 20, 29–31, 42–3, 51–2, 65–7, 72, 91, 134–6, 143 n.11, 149 n.6, 153 n.11
Althusser, L.   147 n.17
anarchism   2, 30, 100, 109, 115, 158 n.17
Anthropocene   114, 117
anti-capitalism   vi–vii, 87–8, 120, 127–8, 131, 133, 135, 138–9, 151 n.1, 152 n.5
Arab Spring   86

Bauer, E.   20, 30, 60, 84
Benjamin, W.   ix, 89
Bloch, E.   ix, 38, 135, 138, 150 n.14
Bonefeld, W.   99, 151 n.1
Bookchin, M.   109–11, 113, 154 n.1
Brecht, B.   79, 148 n.20

capital   29, 33–4, 36–7, 43, 54, 90, 98, 100, 110, 112–17, 119, 145 n.3, 146 n.8, 151 n.4, 153 n.13
capitalism   vii, ix, 1–2, 14, 32–3, 36–39, 41–2, 45, 53, 71, 78, 90–1, 98–9, 108–9, 111–15, 117–19, 121, 123–5, 127–8, 133–5, 145 n.2, 145 n.3, 146 n.8, 146 n.11, 149 n.25, 155 n.4, 157 n.12, 157 n.14, *see also* anti-capitalism
character masks   37, 42, 51, *see also* personification
class   24, 32, 36–8, 41, 46–54, 85, 88, 99, 106, 112–14, 120, 134–5, 138, 143 n.11, 146 n.4, 146 n.6, 147 n.17, 148 n.25, 157 n.12
Cleaver, H.   146 n.5, 147 n.14
climate change   vi, 102–3, 107–108, 114–20, 128–9, 131, 156 n.9

climate justice movement   vii, 118–20, 128
commodity   vii, xi, 32–9, 42, 46, 97, 146 n.7
commoning   95–101, 107, 123–6, 153 n.12, *see also* commons
commons   vii, 95–101, 105, 121–4, 157 n.15, *see also* commoning
communism   vi, ix–x, 15, 32, 38, 49, 54–60, 74, 84–5, 88, 95–6, 105, 126, 133–4, 157 n.12
conversation   16, 18, 27, 100, 104, 106, 123–4, 137, 149 n.8, 154 n.18

De Angelis, M.   97–8
De Beauvoir, S.   29, 145 n.18
Debord, G.   29, 30, 154 n.17
debtor-creditor relation   33–5, 118, 145 n.1, 152 n.10
deep ecology   111–12, 114, 131
democracy   2, 56, 85, 87, 89, 93–4, 103, 121, 126, 152 n.11
dependence   15, 33–5, 68, 97, 113, 118, 120, 125, 143 n.7, *see also* independence
dialectic   vi, 5, 9–10, 125, 144 n.13
Diggers   88–9, 156 n.8
domination   vii, 10, 23, 26, 28–9, 37, 52–3, 90, 110–14, 118, 121, 127, 133, 142 n.4, 143 n.7, 145 n.18, 145 n.3, 153 n.13, 155 n.4, 156 n.9, *see also* hierarchy
Dunayevskaya, R.   126, 146 n.9, 147 n.15, 157 n.14

ecosocialism   109–10, 119
end of history   10–12, 15–18, 20, 74, 143 n.6
Engels, F.   3, 5–6, 84, 95, 125, 127

environment   109, 111, 125, 127–31, 157 n.11, 158 n.17
exchange   32–9, 43, 46–7, 50, 97, 112, 134
exploitation   36–7, 40–2, 78, 97, 118, 142 n.4, *see also* surplus value

Fanon, F.   29, 145 n.18
Federici, S.   98, 129–30, 148 n.25, 153 n.13, 157 n.15
feminism   88, 111, 141 n.3, 145 n.18, 153 n.13
Feuerbach, L.   54, 155 n.3
Fichte, J. G.   45, 148 n.19
Frankfurt School   x, 69, 74, 78, 80–2, 150 n.16
Fraser, N.   65–72, 75–7, 79, 152 n.11
freedom   11–24, 26–7, 33–4, 36, 39, 45, 56, 60, 68, 84, 87–91, 94, 108, 123–4, 126–7, 129, 135, 138, 142 n.3, 143 n.5, 150 n.14, 156 n.6, *see also* self-determination
French Revolution   vi, 6–7, 12, 18–21, 26, 74, 142 n.4

geistige Massen   x, 13–15, 18, 22, 27, 43, 153 n.11, *see also* institutions
Goldman, E.   152 n.8
Graeber, D.   86–7, 94, 141 n.5
green politics   4, 108–13, 119, 121, 128, 130–1

Habermas, J.   74, 150 nn.8–9, 150 n.16
Haitian Revolution   142 n.4
Harvey, D.   100–2, 105, *see also* 'problem of scale'
Hegel, G. W. F.   vi, viii, ix, x, 1–3, 5–32, 43–5, 47, 54, 60–1, 67–8, 71, 73–4, 77, 80, 83–4, 87, 89, 104, 107, 111, 113, 129, 133–5, 137–8
  Phenomenology of Spirit   vi, xi, 4, 6–23, 25–7, 30–2, 42–4, 46, 55–6, 59–60, 62, 71, 81–2, 87, 129, 131, 133–4, 139, 143 n.5, 144 nn.15–16
  Philosophy of Right   6–7, 21–6, 30–31, 72–3, 84, 133–4, 143 n.11, 144 nn.12–16

Hess, M.   30, 84, 155 n.3
hierarchy   3, 7, 20, 38, 85, 88, 100, 102–4, 111, 113, 118, 137, 151 n.3, *see also* domination
history   vi, 8, 10–13, 15, 17–20, 47–8, 54, 73–4, 77, 80, 89, 108, 111, 113–14, 116, 118, 127, 135, 137–8, 156 n.6
Hobbes, T.   116, 120
Holloway, J.   1, 79, 87
Honneth, A.   vi, x, 3, 7, 25, 45, 61–2, 69–81, 134, 149 n.5, 150 n.13
  Freedom's Right   77–8, 149 n.7
  The Idea of Socialism   150 n.15
  normative reconstruction   77–8, 80
  promise of freedom   78, 134
  (with N. Fraser) *Redistribution of Recognition?*   67, 69–72, 74–7, 79, 150 nn.9–10
  spheres of recognition   45, 72–6
  The Struggle for Recognition   69–70, 73
  surplus validity   75–7
horizontalism   x, 2, 85–7, 89, 92, 94–5, 97, 100–2, 124–5, 134, 138, 141 n.5
Horkheimer, M.   69, 81, 115, 136

identity   x, xi, 14, 17, 34, 37, 56, 63–8, 73, 81, 134, 149 n.3
Illich, I.   154 n.18
immanent critique   39, 76, 78, 146 n.7, 150 n.12
independence   15–16, 33–5, 58, 68, 93, 125, *see also* dependence
indigenous struggles   118–19, 126, 128, 157 n.13
Indignados   86
individuality   35, 38, 44–6, 56, 64–5, 75–7, 137
institutions   14, 18, 23–5, 27, 37, 43, 81, 143 n.11, *see also* geistige Massen
inverted world   35, 39, 46, 137, 145 n.2

Klein, N.   91, 120, 130
Kojeve, A.   7, 142 n.3

labour   vii, 14, 33, 36–8, 40–2, 58, 78, 99, 110, 113, 122–3, 127, 142 n.3, 145 n.3, 146 nn.4–6, 148 n.25, 153 n.13, 155 n.5
Lacan, J.   28, 144 n.17
law   14, 23, 34, 44, 53, 70, 73, 121, 150 n.16
Left Hegelianism   vii, x, xi, 4, 6, 20–1, 26, 60, 62, 84, 111, 127, 139, 148 n.24
Lenin, V.   2, 5, 85–6, 106, 152 n.8
liberalism   vi, 23, 25, 40, 63–4, 66, 79–83, 134, 144 n.16, 149 n.1
Locke, J.   122–4, 156 n.10
Luxemburg, R.   2, 85–6, 105–6, 108, 141 n.1

Malm, A.   113–14, 116, 155 n.2
Mann, G. and Wainwright, J.   116–17, 156 n.7
Marcuse, H.   69, 79, 155 n.4
Markell, P.   66–8
market   13–14, 24, 33, 35–7, 42–3, 78, 97, 130
Marx, K.   vi, vii, x, 2–7, 13, 17, 21, 29–61, 74, 79–80, 83–4, 92, 98–9, 107, 109–14, 121–7, 133–4, 137, 141 n.6, 145 nn.2–3, 146 nn.4–6, 146 nn.8–9, 146 n.11, 147 n.15, 147 n.17, 148 n.19, 148 nn.21–3, 152 n.5, 155 nn.2–5, 157 n.11, 157 n.14
   base and superstructure metaphor   48, 52, 59–60, 147 n.16, 148 n.23
   Capital   vii, 35–6, 38, 41–3, 48, 58, 98, 110, 121–2, 124, 133, 145, 146 n.10, 147 n.17, 148 n.19, 156 n.11
   Comments on James Mill   33, 35, 37, 57, 133, 145 n.1
   Economic and Philosophical Manuscripts (1844)   7, 37, 44–5, 54, 59, 133, 146 nn.7–8
   Ethnological Notebooks   126–7
   Grundrisse   33, 41, 43, 58, 133
   On the Jewish Question   44, 57–8
Marx and Engels
   Communist Manifesto   vi, 47, 53, 58
   The German Ideology   38, 57, 84

Marxism-Leninism   100, 105
mastery and slavery   8–10, 12, 28, 113
metabolism   109–10, 114, 123, 125
modernity   74, 77, 80, 150 n.9
money   viii, 34–6, 97
Movement of the Squares   86, 99
multiculturalism   61–72, 80–2, 134, 149 n.2

natural law tradition   45, 95, 122, 147 n.13, 156 n.10
nature   13, 14, 110–13, 115, 122–3, 125, 127–8, 130, 155 n.2, 155 n.5, 156 n.6, 156 nn.10–11, 158 n.16
neoliberalism   1, 4, 7, 21, 27, 32, 35, 62, 83, 98, 115, 133, 138–9

Öcalan, A.   111
Occupy   vi–vii, 2, 82, 86, 88–9, 94, 100, 105, 121, 151 nn.3–4, 152 nn.10–11, 154 n.14
oligarchy   86, 95
Open Marxism   158 n.18
Ostrom, E.   101, 154 n.15

pacifism   91–2, *see also* violence
Pannekoek, A.   115
participation   2, 16, 18, 56, 79, 82, 87, 93–4, 103, 105, 124, 149 n.8
personification   vii, 36–8, 42–3, *see also* character masks
political economy   32, 35–6, 39, 110, 112, 117, 146 n.7, 147 n.13
possessive individualism   41, 45, 96, 120, 124, 138, 147 n.12
precariat   153 n.13
prefiguration   xi, 2–3, 82, 86–9, 91–2, 105, 121, 135–6, 141 nn.2–3, 152 n.5
'problem of organization'   2–3, 85–9, 93, 95, 100–6, *see also* Lenin, V.; Luxemburg, R.
'problem of scale'   3, 95–7, 101–3, 125, 157 n.15, *see also* Harvey, D.

proletariat   38, 41, 50–1, 53, 59, 86, 98, 148 n.25
property   22–3, 32–3, 36, 39–46, 50, 52, 56, 90, 95, 121–4, 126–7, 134, 144 n.12, 147 nn.12–13, 147 n.15, 156 n.10

recognition   vi–xi, 1–22, 24–8, 30–44, 46–8, 51–75, 77, 79–93, 95–8, 100, 102–8, 111, 113, 116–17, 120, 123–39
-contradictory recognition   10–16, 18, 20, 22, 28, 32, 34, 37–40, 42–4, 46, 51–4, 70, 81, 87, 97, 104, 106, 128, 130, 136, 144 n.13, 145 n.1
-institutional recognition   x, 12–16, 18, 22–8, 37, 43, 47, 52–3, 59, 73, 75, 81, 92, 103, 106, 133
-one-sided and unequal recognition   9–11, 13, 34, 37, 41–2, 52–3, 59, 111, 113, 133
-mutual recognition   vi–xi, 1–4, 10, 12, 15–21, 25–8, 30, 32–6, 39–40, 46–7, 54–60, 67–8, 72, 79, 82–96, 98, 106, 108, 116–17, 120, 123–39
reification   vii, 50, 73, *see also* thinghood
Renault, I.   76, 149 n.6
representative democracy   19, 27, 152 n.11, 154 n.14
role definitions   vi–vii, x–xi, 14–16, 25–6, 28, 37–8, 43, 47, 50–3, 58, 72, 91, 93, 135, 137, 146 n.6, 156 n.11
Rousseau, J.-J.   45, 143 n.7, 147 n.13, 152 n.11

Sartre, J.-P.   15, 17, 142 n.2
self-determination   11–12, 16–17, 41, 43, 48, 55–7, 71, 87, 104, 120, 126, 128–30, 135, 137, 139, *see also* freedom
Smith, A.   97
social democracy   1–3, 81, 86, 134, 141 n.6, 142 n.7, 150 n.15
social ecology   109–11, 113
social movements   vii, x–xi, 2–3, 82, 86–95, 99–100, 105–6
spontaneity   19, 106
Stirner, M.   21, 29–30, 60, 84
surplus value   41–2, *see also* exploitation

Taylor, C.   vi, 3, 61–6, 69, 81, 134, 149 n.1, 149 nn.3–4
technology   109, 114–15, 155 n.4
thinghood   44, 50, 53, *see also* reification
Thompson, E. P.   96, 101
Tully, J.   66–8

violence   91–2, 99, 119, *see also* pacifism

Weber, M.   74, 150 n.9

Young-Hegelianism, *see* Left-Hegelianism

Zapatistas   x–xi
Zibechi, R.   99, 102, 104–6
Zizek, S   144 n.17